First things first

First Things First

© copyright 2010 by Michael Jobling

ISBN 978-0-9565818-2-2

All rights reserved.

No part of this publication may be reproduced or transmitted in any form or by any means, electronic or mechanical, including photocopy, recording or any information storage or retrieval system, without permission in writing from the author.

Published by Treasure House Creative, Milton Keynes

Take another look

The first eleven chapters of the Bible are the subject of much controversy. Atheist fundamentalists see them as useless legends with no relevance for today while religious fundamentalists view them as divinely inspired, historical truth. In between, a spectrum of bemused believers and confused agnostics shrug their shoulders, wonder for a moment and get on with the here and now.

In my opinion, the arguments between those at each end of the spectrum, focusing as they do solely on whether these narratives are real historical events, miss the point. It's a fair question, but not the most important one. To really make sense of Genesis 1–11, I believe, you must approach these narratives, not as history or science but as art. You need to look at them through the eyes of a writer or a dramatist, a painter or a sculptor. It's only when you approach these documents with a creative mind that they come to life, yielding fabulous treasures of wisdom and insight, challenging our own outlook and culture and posing the essential question, "Where does human creativity come from?"

That's not to say that it doesn't matter whether these events really happened. But we need to allow for the fact that these writings come from a culture that didn't draw a rigid line between allegory and history and whose understanding of what is true and not true was different to ours.

Whatever scientific or religious baggage you bring with you, I invite you to put it down and to approach these writings with new eyes as if you had never seen them or heard of them before. You might be in for a surprise.

Come with me and enjoy a journey to the dawn of time.

Michael Jobling

Finding your way around

Each chapter of this book has three ingredients which are clearly signposted:

Scripture
I've gone back to the Hebrew Bible and translated it (or in some cases paraphrased it) for myself. Here I've tried to follow the original narrative closely and not to let my imagination run away with me. To make these sections distinct I've put them in a different font.

Imagine
These sections are my attempt to bring the Bible text to life, filling in some gaps in the process. I hope you find these sections enjoyable and helpful but it is important to understand that these sections come from my imagination. I've tried to be faithful to the Bible text and to draw in some archaeological insights in the process. But take it with a pinch of salt. The events may not have happened the way I describe. I might have got it wrong. If you imagine it differently, that's fine.

Information
Alongside the text you'll also find some information boxes which explain some of the background to help your understanding and keep your imagination on track.

New Testament links
At the end of some chapers you'll find a list of any passages in the New Testament that refer back to that section of Genesis.

Contents

Page no

1	In the first place	7
2	The first man	15
3	The first woman	23
4	The first murder	37
5	The first city	45
6	The first man dies	51
7	The first superheroes	57
8	The first ocean voyage	63
9	The first covenant	77
10	The first drunk	83
11	The first empire	93
12	The first communication crisis	97
13	Life flows on	103
14	First step on the road to the promised land	109
	Group notes: Stories from the dawn of time	115
	Group notes: Noah and now	123
	Sources	129

Chapter 1

In the first place

The account of the heavens and the earth when they were created

Imagine

Come with me as I step into an imaginary time machine and take you back to Mesopotamia (Iraq) somewhere around 2,000 years BC. We find ourselves on a dusty street in a town constructed from whitewashed brick buildings. Through the open door of one of the houses we glimpse a man seated at a table. We greet him and he invites us in. He's holding a piece of reed in his hand and he's pressing it into a rectangular piece of wet clay, covering it with little triangular marks.

"What are you doing?" we ask.

"This is the latest technology," he tells us. "It's called writing. It's going to change the world. Each symbol represents a sound and, when you make the sounds, it talks to you. It tells you things."

Fascinated, we watch. When he's completely covered the piece of clay with triangular marks, he leaves it in the sun to dry. When it's hard, he slips it into a case, itself made from dried clay. He smears some wet clay on the outside and writes a short sentence.

"What does that say?" we ask. He reads it back to us,

"This is the written account of Adam's Line." He says. "We put that on the outside so we know what's inside. Saves us wearing away the writing by constantly taking it out and putting it back. And it makes it easier to find the one you want."

"What about this other one?" we ask, pointing to another clay case on another table nearby.

> **Information**
> **Clay tablets**
>
> The first eleven chapters of Genesis were almost certainly first written on clay tablets and then incorporated into the book of Genesis at a later date. The custom was to place the clay tablet into a clay sleeve (the way we put a CD into a CD case). A brief sentence on the outside of the sleeve would describe the contents of the document inside. Much later, when the clay documents were merged into a papyrus roll, the sentences from the sleeves were incorporated into the text. See the following verses:
>
> Genesis 2 v 4, 5 v 1, 6 v 9, 10 v 1, 10 v 31, 10 v 32, 11 v 10, 11 v 27.

"This is the account of the heavens and the earth when they were created", he reads from the cover. "That's an amazing piece of writing."

"What is it, a story?" We ask. "More than a story," he says. "It's a beautifully constructed work of art."

"A picture?"

"In a manner of speaking. A picture in words. It's full of word patterns."

"Like a poem?"

"Sort of. You might call it a word sculpture. I tell you what, let me take it out and read it to you."

Scripture (Genesis 1 v 1–2 v 3)

The most important thing is, God has been creating the Heavens and the Earth.

The Earth is empty and shapeless; darkness has been covering the depths of space and the wind of God has been moving across the liquid depths,

And God has been saying:

"Let light be!" So light is.

God has been looking at the light. It's good.

And God has been making a distinction between the light and the darkness.

He's called the light "day",
And the darkness he's called "night".

So there's been an evening and a morning. Day one.

And God has been saying:

"Let there be a boundary between the waters to divide one set of water from the other."

And God's making a boundary to divide the waters below from the waters above, And that's how it is.

God's calling the boundary "the sky".

Information
In the beginning

Most translations of Genesis 1 start with the words "In the beginning."

The word translated "beginning" is related to the Hebrew word for "head" and also to the number one. It's the "head place", the "number one position". It can mean first in time, but it can also mean first in importance. That's why I've translated it "The most important thing is..."

So there's been an evening and a morning. Day two.

God has been saying:
"Let the water below the sky gather together into one place
And let dry land appear." And that's how it is.

God's called the dry land "land" and the gathered waters "sea".
He's been looking at it. It's good.

Information
Hebrew Verbs

Ancient Hebrew does not have the same concept of past, present and future as modern English. We ask "When did it happen? Is it going on now, is it in the past, is it still yet to happen in the future?" Ancient Hebrew isn't interested in time. It stands outside of time, if you like, and views things from a timeless perspective. Instead of asking, when did this happen? it asks, "Does the action have an end or does it go on indefinitely?" and "How forceful is it?" The perfect tense, used for actions that have an end, often does the job of our past tense but it can also represent an action in the past, present or future which is not going to go on indefinitely. Most of the verbs in Genesis 1 are in the perfect tense.

With the Hebrew tenses in mind, there have been people as long ago as the 4th century AD who have understood Genesis 1 as saying that God *is* creating the world rather than that he *has* created it and also that the process of creation will eventually reach a point of completion – it will not continue indefinitely. Given the absence of past, present and future in Hebrew verbs, this understanding is legitimate. Following this interpretation you can place the world in which we live today within day six, with the seventh day still to come in the future, representing the coming age after the resurrection and the final judgement.

In the first place

And God has been saying:

"Let the earth sprout every kind of grass, herbs, vegetables, trees and plants that bear seed, fruit and flowers." And that's how it is. The Earth has sprouted every kind of greenery, vegetables, seed-bearing plants and fruit-bearing trees according to their species.

God's been looking at it. It's good.

So there's been an evening and a morning. Day three.

And God's been saying:

"Let there be lights in the sky to distinguish between day and night and to give warning, to signal the time for festivals and to mark off the days and months and to shed light on the earth." And that's how it is.

God's been making the orbits of the sun and moon, the sun to control the day and the moon to control the night. God's been providing them to shine on the earth and to control day and night and to distinguish between light and darkness.

God's been looking at it. It's good.

So there's been an evening and a morning. Day four.

God's been saying:

"Let the waters teem with shoals of living things and let birds fly over the earth against the sky."

And God's been making the great sea monsters and all kinds of things which crawl in the water and every kind of winged bird.

He's been looking at it. It's good.

God's been blessing them and saying:

"Be fruitful and increase in numbers. Fill the waters in the seas and fly all over the earth."

So there's been an evening and a morning. Day five.

And God's been saying:

"Let the earth produce various kinds of intelligent creatures: cattle and reptiles and living creatures of different kinds." And that's how it is. God's making every kind of living creature on the earth, every kind of cattle and every reptile that lives on the land.

God's been looking at it. It's good.

And God's been saying:

"Let us make mankind to reflect and resemble us and let them rule over the fish in the sea and the birds in the sky and over the cattle – over all the earth and everything that moves on the earth."

And God's been making mankind to reflect him. He's been making them like God. He's been making them male and female.

God's been blessing them and saying to them:

"Be fruitful and grow in numbers. Rule the earth and bring it under your control. Rule over the fish in the sea and the birds in the sky and over all the living things which move on the earth."

And God's been saying:

"See, I have given you all the seed-bearing plants on the face of the earth and all the trees which bear fruit, to be your food. And to all the living creatures on earth, the birds in the sky and every thing that moves and has a soul, I am giving them all the green herbs and vegetables to eat."

And that's how it is.

God's been looking at everything he has been making and it's extremely good.

There's an evening and a morning. Day six.

So the heavens and the Earth and the host of things they contain are being created by God.

And on the seventh day God is resting from all the work he has been doing.

So God is blessing the seventh day and making it special because in it he is resting from all he's been doing.

Information
The days

2 Peter 2 v 8, says "with the Lord a day is like a thousand years and a thousand years are like a day". That has led some Christian commentators to conclude that these days are not literal but represent phases of God's activity. The way the days are arranged suggests that the author is not referring to strict 24 hour periods. For example, Day 1 sees the creation of light but the sources of light are not created until day 4. The first three days set the stage, the next three bring on the actors. Day 2 sees the separation of sea and sky; the creatures that inhabit sea and sky appear on day 5. Day 3 sees the creation of dry land; the plants and living creatures that live on the land appear in day 6.

The passage of evening and morning and the passing of the days form a refrain that breaks up the narrative, perhaps telling us that the earth God has created constantly circles through day and night and that time is part of the created order.

New Testament Links

These passages in the New Testament refer back to Genesis chapter 1:

Luke 6 v 9
Romans 1 v 18 – 23
Colossians 1 v 16
Hebrews 4 v 1-9

Luke 13 v 16
Ephesians 2 v 10
1 Timothy 4 v 4
Revelation 4 v 11

Chapter 2

The first man
The written account of Adam's Line (Part 1)

Scripture (Genesis 2 v 4–17)

Yahweh God formed a man out of clay from the earth and he blew the spirit of life into his nose and he became a living, feeling, thinking being.

This was before Yahweh God had caused the shrubs and the vegetation on the earth to spring up. Yahweh God had not given any rain to the earth and mankind was not there to cultivate it but a mist used to rise from the land to moisten the surface of the ground.

Yahweh God had planted an enclosed garden in Eden, towards the east, and there he put the man he had made.

Yahweh God caused all kinds of trees that were pleasant to look at and good to eat to shoot up from the earth. In the middle of the garden was the tree of life, alongside the tree of the knowledge of good and evil.

A stream went out from Eden to water the garden and there it separated and became the source of four rivers. The name of the first is Pishon; it winds through all the land of Havilah where there is gold (there is good quality gold in that land as well as bdellium and onyx). The name of the second river is Gishon, it winds through the whole land of Cush. The name of the third river is Hidekkel (= the Tigris), this goes to the East of Assyria. The fourth one is the Euphrates.

**Information
Eden**

Is the garden real or symbolic? It is difficult to tell. There are geographical references which suggest it was a real place. One Biblical archaeologist, David Rohl, has used the details of the rivers mentioned in the Biblical account to locate the Garden of Eden in the Adjichay Valley, an area in Northern Iran, near the border with Armenia. On the other hand, the tree of life and the tree of the fruit of the knowledge of good and evil are clearly allegorical. They are evidently not real trees. These trees represent possibilities that are open to the man and the woman in the garden.

Traditionally, Jews and Christians have seen this as a real historical story about the first man and woman that God created. However, it can be seen as the story of every married couple. The phrase "everything in the garden is lovely" describes the way many newlyweds feel about their relationship. But we all have a snake in our garden and too often we end up spoiling things for ourselves. You can also see the story as an allegory of the condition of the whole human race. The garden can represent the whole planet. Adam is every man and Eve is every woman. Our thirst for knowledge and power has destroyed the paradise we could be living in.

The first man

Yahweh God took the man and placed him in the Garden of Eden to cultivate and guard it. And he issued a decree to the man: "You may eat freely of all the trees of the garden but do not eat from the fruit of the tree of the knowledge of good and evil for when you eat it you will certainly die."

Information
Adam

The name Adam is the Hebrew word for "Man". There are two words for man in Hebrew, "ish" which is used for man as distinct from the animals and "adam" which is man as distinct from woman. The word "adam" is also closely related to the Hebrew words for "red" and "soil" which is why in the "Imagine" section, I call Adam "Red".

There seem to be two accounts of the creation of mankind in Genesis. The one in Genesis 1 describes how God created the human race in general. The one in Genesis 2 is about the creation of a particular man who may or may not be the first. The text implies that Adam was the first man but also that he was specially created separately to the rest of mankind referred to in Genesis 1 v 26 and 27.

While Genesis is very specific in stating that God created (or is creating) mankind, it is not too specific about the process by which he did (or is doing) it. In the ancient Hebrew mind everything that happens is God's doing, so there is no problem with seeing God's hand at work in evolution and there is room for all the stages of evolution within Genesis 1 verse 26 and 27 and equally within Genesis 2 v 7.

Imagine

He opened his eyes.

As they focused he could see an intricate pattern of interlocking shapes in various shades of green, lit by the morning sun and fluttering with a continuous movement against an azure blue sky.

He sat up and looked around.

The interlocking shapes were attached to tall, greyish, brownish, greenish columns that stood all around him, rooted in the ground.

He crawled towards one and put his hand on it. Crawling over the bare earth was painful, so, putting his hand against the column, he hauled himself up onto his legs and discovered he could stand.

Something was hanging down from a low branch of the tree. Instinctively, he reached out to grab it. He looked at it, smelt it, tasted it, bit into it. The sweet juice trickled down his throat and down his cheek. It was pleasant.

He began to walk about and explore his surroundings. He found a stream, quenched his thirst and enjoyed splashing in the water. He soon became aware that there were other beings sharing this environment with him – little ones that flitted to and fro and hid among the complicated shapes at the top of the columns. There were bigger ones too that barged about in the undergrowth, cracking twigs under their feet and making fearsome snorting and moaning noises.

The air became hot and he lay down in the shade and slept.
When he woke up it was cooler. The light had changed. Instead of

The first man

coming from above it was shining from the side, creating long shadows. Everywhere was full of noise. He could hear the stream rushing and the wind whispering and all the beings around him hooting and growling and twittering. But then he heard the Voice.

Unlike the other sounds, it came from within him, resonating in his heart and his head, instead of his ears.

"Hey! Red!" it seemed to say. He looked around. He could see green things and brown things and white things, blue things and yellow things. He noticed his hands. They were kind of red. So were his legs. He was red. Was the Voice talking to him?

He listened.

The voice seemed to know he was paying attention.

"How do you like my garden?" It asked.

"It's good," he replied.

"I've placed you here to cultivate and guard it. I'm going to meet with you each evening to show you what I want you to do. I'm giving you all the fruit of all the trees for your food. You may eat freely of them but be warned, the fruit of the tree of the knowledge of good and evil is dangerous. Don't eat from that one for, if you do, it will kill you."

New Testament Link

There is an allusion to the garden of Eden in Revelation 2 v 7

Scripture (Genesis 2 v 18–20)

Yahweh God said, "It isn't good for the man to be on his own. I will make him a suitable helper."

And Yahweh God sent all the wild animals and all the birds from the sky and brought them to the man to see what he would call them. And whatever the man called each living creature, that was its name. The man gave names to all the domestic animals, the birds of the sky and the wild animals. But he didn't find a suitable helper for him.

Imagine

A shaft of light pierced through the green canopy above him and shone on his face. Red woke, stretched, yawned, stood up, relieved the pressure in his bladder, looked around and set about finding something good to eat on the trees in the garden and quenching his thirst from the waters of the stream.

His thirst quenched and his hunger sated, he continued to explore the garden. He wanted to find out more about the other creatures. Some were shy and he had to stay very still to watch them, otherwise they ran off into the undergrowth or up into the treetops. Others were inquisitive and came to him. Some were tiny and crawled all over him. He had to be careful not to crush them under his feet as he walked. He spent ages watching a caterpillar eating a leaf and a butterfly sticking its long nose into the flowers. Then his attention was taken by a couple of birds hopping about in the branches of a tree. He sat down on a rock while he looked upwards to watch them. Suddenly, he felt something wet against his bare leg and looked down to find a brown, furry, four legged creature with a wagging tail sniffing at his knee. The creature backed off and ran round him in a circle before coming up and nuzzling his leg with its nose once more. He patted the animal and it backed off and started making a noise while fixing him intently with its gaze. Red tried to imitate the noise it made,

"Dogh! dogh dogh!" was the nearest he could make to the sound. The animal seemed to understand and barked back. Idly, Red picked up a piece of wood from the floor and threw it into the undergrowth. The creature ran after it, brought it back and dropped it down at Red's feet. "Dogh! dogh!" it said again and seemed to be saying, "do it again." They continued the game for a while. "I'm going to call you 'dog'," Red said. Dog wagged his tail.

Over a period of several days, Red continued to have encounters with new animals and to give them names. He tried jumping on the back of some of the larger ones. Some allowed him to ride them. One gave him an exhilarating, high speed gallop up through the trees onto the grassland on an open hilltop. Dog ran alongside, yapping excitedly at the animal's feet. Red tried to imitate the snorting sound. The nearest he could get was "Horse!"

Birds came to land on his shoulder or his outstretched arm. He stuck his face in the clear waters of a lake, opened his eyes and found himself eye to eye with a scaly creature with fins. It opened and closed its mouth. Red did the same but choked as he inadvertently started to breath in water. "Fish!" He said, as he squirted the water out of his mouth.

Chapter 3

The first woman
The written account of Adam's Line (Part 2)

Scripture (Genesis 2 v 21–24)

Jahweh God caused a deep slumber to fall on the man and he fell asleep. He took one of the man's ribs and closed up the flesh under it. He built up the rib which he took from the man and made it into a woman. Then he brought her to the man. The man said,

"This time she is bone from my bone and flesh from my flesh. She will be called woman because she was taken from man."

Because of this a man will leave his father and mother and be bonded to his woman and they will become one flesh.

Information

The famous Victorian Bible scholar, Matthew Henry, commented on this passage that Eve was:
"not taken from Adam's head to top him, nor from his feet to be trampled on by him but from his side to be equal with him, under his arm to be protected by him and near his heart to be loved."

Imagine

For several months, Red continued getting to know the other creatures, marvelling at the diversity of their shapes and colours, studying their diets and habitats, analysing and imitating their calls. He began to realise that, with almost all of them, there were two forms. He observed how the two forms attracted each other, sometimes by displays of colour and dance, sometimes by scent and song. He watched how they mated, how the females had young. He watched the young suckle milk from their mothers and, with some of the larger creatures, he had a go himself, developing a taste for warm, fatty cow's milk.

Normally, Red slept on a soft, mossy bank at the foot of a tree. He would settle down to sleep after the sun had set and normally he would wake when a shaft of sunlight shone through a gap in the leaves above him and touched his face.

This morning, though, he woke before the sun shone, while it was still dark.

Something slightly heavy was pressing on the left side of his chest. He tried to move his left arm to feel what it was but the arm was pinned to his side; he couldn't move it. He lifted his right hand and reached over to feel his chest. His hand touched strands of something smooth and soft. He ran his fingers through them. His hands followed the grain of the soft hairy stuff until it ended and his hand described an elegant curve downwards following a soft mound of warm skin. What was it? What had happened to him during the night? As his hand made contact with his own body he realised that the hair and skin were not part of him but belonged to something else lying on top of him. He slid his hand along the join, feeling where the other creature's body made contact with his. Its skin felt beautifully smooth and soft, unlike his own rough hairiness. There seemed to be an arm lying across his chest and a head above it, just below his chin.

It was breathing, whatever it was. He could feel its warm breath on his shoulder and its back rising and falling slightly under his hand. He gently tried to move from under it. It stirred slightly and rolled to the left, enabling him to gently extricate his arm and to sit up beside the new creature, which continued to sleep.

Slowly, the dawn broke and, as the light returned, he began to distinguish the creature's shape. An astonishing thought crept into his mind. "It's a female version of me!" It wasn't an ape – he'd seen some of them. They were a bit like him but hairy and rough and boisterous. This creature had only the lightest down of hair on its skin and a huge mane of soft hair that fell in wavy strands around its neck and over its body. The hair fell over two mounds of flesh and what he guessed were nipples – like those he'd seen on the females of other creatures. It stirred and opened its eyes, the largest and most intelligent eyes he had yet seen. Its mouth opened and she spoke.

Information
One flesh

The account of the creation of Adam and Eve ("Red" and "Life Mother") forms the basis of the Jewish and Christian view of marriage. Both Jesus and Paul refer back to it when they teach about marriage in the New Testament. The Bible pattern is one man and one woman bonded to each other for life. Marriage is not created by the state, the church or the law – none of these existed at this stage in the human story. It's the commitment, the decision to "leave and cleave" that creates a marriage in God's eyes.

"Hello!"

Each evening, he'd heard the Voice, held conversations with it. But this was different. This voice wasn't inside him; it came from her, dripping like honey from her parted lips. With the Voice he didn't have to talk back. The Voice understood what he was thinking. This creature didn't show any sign of reading his mind, so he spoke.

"Hello", he replied, "Who are you?"

"I don't know", she replied, "Who would you like me to be?"

In that moment, he heard the Voice,

"I've made her to be your companion and helper. Treat her well."

New Testament Links

You'll find references to the creation of Eve in the New Testament in:

Matthew 19 v 4–6
Mark 10 v 2–9
1 Corinthians 6 v 16
Ephesians 5 v 28–32

Scripture (Genesis 2 v 25–3 v 6)

The two of them were naked [or clever] but not ashamed.

Now the snake was the most naked [clever] of all the wild animals that Yahweh God had made and he said to the woman,

"Is it true that God told you not to eat from any tree in the garden?"

The woman said, "We can eat the fruit from all the trees in the garden. But Yahweh God said to us "Don't eat from the tree which is in the middle of the garden and don't touch it, in case you die."

And the snake said to the woman,

"You won't die. God knows that as soon as you eat from it your eyes will be opened and you will become like God knowing good and evil."

The woman saw that the tree was good for food and pleasant to look at and desirable to give wisdom and she took some of the fruit and ate it …

Information
Naked and cunning

The whole of this story turns on a pun in the original Hebrew. The words for "naked" and "cunning" sound almost the same. The snake is naked because it doesn't have fur but it is cunning, too. Adam and Eve are naked – clothes haven't been invented. More importantly the nakedness is a symbol of openness, honesty and intimacy. Nothing comes between them and there is nothing they hide from each other. But by eating the fruit they exchange nakedness for cunning. They begin to feel the need to hide from each other, to deceive and trick each other. Part of the art of marriage is in laying aside cunning and deceit in order to discover and nurture total openness.

Imagine

They were sitting by a stream, bathing their feet in the cool water. She was cradling a baby rabbit in her arms. "You're so caring and nurturing," he said. You want to care for everything, including me."

She smiled, "I just love looking after things. Some need more looking after than others – especially you!" She playfully kicked her feet in the water and splashed it over him.

It made such a difference, having someone to share things with. They had been inseparable for days. They had laughed together at the antics of some of the other creatures, gasped together at the view from a hilltop, raced each other, chased each other, hugged each other and kissed each other. Their eyes shone with love whenever they looked at each other. Each evening they thanked the Voice for the gift he had given them of each other.

The Voice continued to meet them each evening as the sun dropped towards the horizon and cool breezes rustled the leaves on the trees. She could hear the Voice too – Red compared notes with her and they reminded each other afterwards what the Voice had told them. The Voice answered questions that were in their minds, gave them instructions for the next day's activity.

They talked endlessly about the things they saw and the things that happened each day in the garden and about the emotions and sensations they felt. Much of the time their feelings and reactions were the same. But they also discovered there were some things they saw differently. In some situations they reacted in different ways. Life Mother sometimes seemed to have eyes in the back of her head; an ability to take in information from several directions at once. Red was more focused. He could get lost in watching

The first woman

something, focusing all his attention on one thing and blotting out everything else.

Perhaps that's why she saw the snake and he didn't. He had become totally absorbed in a project he was planning, drawing a plan in the sand of a beach at the side of a stream. She noticed the snake out of the corner of her eye at first. He was oblivious to it.

It wasn't actually a snake. She didn't know what it was but there was something snake-like about it, something that reminded her of the slithery, scaly, beautiful sinuous creatures they'd seen in the garden. So she called it a snake, when she eventually told Red about it.

To her surprise, it began to talk to her.

"So, God's forbidden you to eat from the trees in the garden, I hear?" It said, fixing her with one eye in a hypnotic gaze.

"Oh no," she replied, "We can eat from all the trees, except the one in the centre of the garden. "It's just that one. It's for our protection. The Voice says we'll die if we even touch it."

"Oh, no you won't!" the snake smiled. "God's just told you that to trick you. Haven't you realised why the fruit is called the fruit of the knowledge of good and evil? It's because it will make you wise. It will make you like God. He doesn't want you to be a threat to him, that's why he's forbidden you to eat from it. You think he's trying to protect you, don't you? But really, he just wants to make you his prisoners.

"Look, I've got some of the fruit of that tree here. I've eaten some myself and I'm still alive. Its taste is amazing, like nothing you've ever tasted before. It makes your sight really clear. When you've eaten it you can see into the future; you can see the future consequences of your actions; how useful is that? Instead of relying on God to tell you what to do, you can work it out for yourselves. It makes you clever. Here, why not taste some, now?"

She hesitated. "I don't ... she began."

"Don't tell me you're afraid!" the snake taunted her. "You didn't strike me as a scaredy cat. I'd got you down as someone who's up for an adventure and willing to try new things."

"It's not that I'm afraid," she said, "I don't want to try it without Red, my companion. We do everything together."

"Well, take some for him. Try it together when he's finished his little project."

The hypnotic eyes continued to bore into her. She capitulated. "Alright then. Leave some with me, we'll try it later."

The snake slithered away. The two pieces of fruit lay on a rock. The sun moved round in the sky. It was midday. She was hungry. Gingerly, she reached out and touched the fruit.

Nothing happened. She was still alive. She picked it up. Smelt it. It was fragrant and appealing. She put it to her mouth. It tasted good.

> **Information**
> **What was Adam doing?**
>
> Before I started to write this part of the book I had always assumed that Adam was somewhere else while Eve talked to the serpent. I was surprised to find the verse that says she gave Adam some of the fruit because he was with her. Adam was there all the time.
>
> Did he not see the serpent? Did he allow the whole conversation to go on without doing anything to interrupt? Was his attention focused elsewhere?
>
> I've imagined what might have happened. But it's only a guess.

The first woman

Impulsively, she bit into it.

The snake was right. It changed the way she saw things. It was like experiencing another dimension.

She saw the Voice being angry. She saw it turning her out of the garden, creating a new companion for Red in her place, banishing her to wander in the wastelands beyond the garden, alone forever. She saw herself growing old, becoming weak and dying alone.

Then she saw herself giving the fruit to Red. They would both be shut out of the garden then. But at least she wouldn't be alone. The thought of being without him was unbearable.

She had to get him to eat it too.

Scripture (Genesis 3 v 6–24)

She ate it and also gave some to her husband, who also ate. Then their eyes were opened and they knew that they were naked [clever] and they sewed fig leaves together and made themselves aprons.

Then they heard the voice of Yahweh God as he moved through the garden in the coolness of the evening and the man and his wife hid from Yahweh's face among the trees in the garden. Yahweh God called to the man and said to him,

"Where are you?"

And he said, "I heard your voice in the garden and I was afraid because I was naked [clever] and I hid."

And God said,

"Who showed you that you were naked [clever]? Or have you eaten from the fruit that I commanded you not to eat from?"

The man said, "The woman you gave me to keep me company, she gave me some of the fruit and I ate it."

Then Yahweh God said to the woman,

"Why did you do this?"

And the woman said, "The snake led me astray and I ate it."
Then Jahweh God said to the snake,

"Because you have done this you are cursed among the domestic and wild animals. You alone of all of them will move on your belly and eat dust all the days of your life. I will put enmity between you and the woman and between your descendant and her descendants. He will wound your head and you will wound his heel."

To the woman he said,

"I am going to greatly increase your labour and sorrow. You are going to bear children in pain yet still desire your husband, and he will rule over you."

And to the man he said,

"Because you listened to what your wife said and ate some of the fruit which I told you not to eat, the earth is going to be cursed because you are on it.

> **Information**
>
> Notice how Adam and Eve pass the buck. He blames her, she blames the serpent. They are using their new found cunning to try to escape God's condemnation – but in vain.

"You will have to go through pain to get something to eat all the days of your life. The earth will produce thorns and brambles for you and you will have to eat green vegetables. You will eat them with a sweaty face until you go back to the earth, for that's where you were taken from. Dust is what you are and dust is what you will return to,"

The man named his wife "Mother of Life" because she was the mother of everyone who lives. And Yahweh God made animal-skin tunics for the man and his wife and clothed them. Yahweh God said, "Look. The man has become one of us, knowing good and evil. Now, in case he reaches out and takes fruit from the tree of life and eats it…"

And Yahweh God sent them out of the garden of Eden to cultivate the earth as they took possession of it from there. And he drove the man out and made him live to the east of the garden of Eden. He put there the cherubs and the flaming sword that turns about to guard the path to the tree of life.

Imagine

He could tell that something had happened as soon as he turned to look at her. There was a different look in her eyes. He couldn't see into her soul the way he had done before. It was as if she was hiding something from him.

"What's wrong?" Was the first thing he asked.

"Nothing; I'm fine," she said. "I found this fantastic new fruit. You'll love it. Here, try some."

The thought that she would not be honest with him never crossed his mind. He took it, put it in his mouth and chewed on it.

He knew something was different, straightaway. He suddenly saw her, not as a blessing but a threat. Not as a companion but as a resource. He realised he had to be careful. She was useful to him, this woman. But she had power over him. He had to tread carefully so that she didn't control him.

Shame came into the picture too. Each of them felt guilty, she for her disobedience, he for his neglect. Trying to cover their outward nakedness was a symbol of the shame they felt. But it was also an expression of their new cunning. He knew that the physical desire he had for her was his weak point. She would be able to manipulate that to get what she wanted. He could foresee situations where he would respond to the desire and she would rebuff him. The rejection would scour the inside of his soul.

"I'd like you to cover yourself up." He said. I can't go on being aroused all the time. And I'm going to cover myself too."
It seemed logical to her. She didn't want to be just a sex object. She wanted him to love her soul, not just her body.

In the evening, the Voice came. They were afraid and tried to hide but couldn't.

New Testament Links

The tree of life
The tree of life is referred to in:
Revelation 2 v 7
Revelation 22 v 2, 14 and 19

The serpent
There are references to Satan as a serpent in 2 Corinthians 11 v 3 and Revelation 12 v 9

Information

The tree symbolises something to do with knowing good and evil. The fruit must therefore be something that the knowledge of good and evil brings about or makes possible. Knowing what is good and what is evil makes us responsible for our actions and therefore subject to blame when we choose what is evil.

Adam and Eve's sin was more than just eating the fruit. The root of it lay in what this meant for their relationship with God. Eating the fruit was an act of disobedience and rebellion against God. Even worse, underlying the disobedience was a failure to trust God. That's where the sin really lay. The whole of the Bible emphasises the importance of responding to God with faith. The serpent tempted Eve to doubt God. She gave in to the temptation and Adam evidently followed suit.

Theologians agree that Adam and Eve's sin has an enduring effect on the rest of the human race, sometimes referred to as "original sin". The reformer John Calvin described this as, "The hereditary depravity and corruption of our nature, extending to all parts of the soul, which in the first place makes us deserving of the wrath of God and in the next place produces in us those works which the scripture calls the works of the flesh."

New Testament Links

Adam and Eve
There are references to Adam and Eve's sin in: Romans 5 v 12; 1 Corinthians 15 v 22 and v 45 and 1 Timothy 2 v 13–14.

Information
The curse

It's important to make a distinction between curse and law. Both are pronounced by God and both can be resisted but the law is binding in a way that a curse isn't. We can disobey God's law but we always face the consequences. A curse has a negative influence but we are not bound by it and will be blessed if we work against it. We can't use a curse as an excuse; we are still responsible for our actions.

As a result of the curse the environment turns against mankind and making a living becomes hard and painful. Men dominate women and yet women still long to be cherished by them. It's a description of the human condition that we recognise too well. But it can be resisted. Men don't have to dominate women and work doesn't have to be hard and painful. The curse on the serpent is that the woman's seed would bruise his head. Christians see that as foreshadowing the victory that Jesus (the son of a woman) has obtained over the serpent (Satan). As the effects of Jesus' victory work out, the curse can in part be undone. Men can learn to become like Jesus and lift women up rather than putting them down. Women can serve their men for Jesus' sake without being rebellious and resentful and, through the power of the Holy Spirit, work can become a creative joy again.

New Testament Links

The curse
Revelation 22 v 3 looks forward to a time when the curse God announced in the Garden of Eden will be lifted.

Chapter 4

The first murder
The written account of Adam's Line (Part 3)

Scripture (Genesis 4 v 1–2)

And the man had sex with Mother of Life, his woman, and she conceived and gave birth to Produce. She said, "I have produced a man with Jahweh's help." And once more she gave birth to his brother, Mist.

Imagination

She screamed with the pain. Red tried to comfort her. He felt helpless, seeing her in such agony. The physical pain seemed to be accompanied by a deep, angry determination within her. She directed the anger at him. "It's your fault," she said, "You did this to me!" But she clung onto his arm, her fingernails digging into his flesh as another contraction came and she screamed again.

He knew what was happening. It had all started after they'd been driven from the garden. Full of fear, they had clung to each other in the darkness of their first night outside of paradise. "Can you ever forgive me?" She had said. "I've spoilt everything. I had to give you the fruit because if I hadn't I would have been thrown out alone."

"I should have been looking out for you." He said "We're still in Jahweh's world, if not in the garden. It's a good world. We can make our own garden. You'll see." In the darkness he had sought her lips. They'd clung to each other and in the passion that their closeness aroused he'd done to her what he'd seen the animals do.

"It's coming out!" she gasped, "Look!" Red gently pulled the little human from between Life Mother's legs. He lifted it up and placed it in her arms. The screaming had stopped. She looked weary and weak but a huge smile spread across her face as she met the face of her son eye to eye.

"With God's help I've produced a man!" She said. "Hello, Produce! Aren't you a fine little fellow!"

Scripture
(Genesis 4 v 2–8)

It came about that Mist tended flocks of animals while Produce worked the land. And Produce took some of the produce of his work and went to give it to Jahweh as an offering. At the same time Mist brought with him the firstborn and the very best of his herds. Jahweh rescued Mist because of his offering but he did not rescue Produce. Produce was very angry and his face fell.

Information

The name "Cain" comes from a Hebrew verb that can mean to create, produce, acquire or buy. Eve gives Cain his name, expressing her joy but also evidently viewing the child as her possession.

The name Abel comes from a verb that has two related meanings. One is to do with mist or vapour. The secondary meaning is to do with vanity or foolishness. We're not told who gave him his name or why. He was the wiser of the two brothers, hence not foolish, but he died young, murdered by his brother. The name "mist" or "vapour" may relate to the brevity of his time on earth.

The first murder

Jahweh said to him, "Why are you angry? Why the long face? If you do good, you will be lifted up. If you don't do good, sin is lying in wait for you at your door. It wants to overwhelm you but you must master it."

But Produce said to his brother Mist "Let's go to the fields." And Produce rose up against Mist and killed him.

And Jahweh said to Produce, "Where's your brother – Mist?"
He said, "I don't know; am I my brother's minder?"
And Jahweh said, "What have you done? The voice of your brother's blood is crying out to me from the ground. Look, you are under a curse and driven from the ground which has opened its mouth to receive your brother's blood from your hand. If you cultivate the land, it won't produce any wealth for you. You'll have to wander the earth as a rootless runaway."

And Cain said to the Lord, "This is a severe punishment for me. You are driving me today from enjoying the soil and hiding me from your presence. I'm going to be a rootless runaway in the earth and anyone who meets me is going to kill me."

And Yahweh said, "That won't happen, because anyone who kills Cain will receive Cain's punishment seven times over." And Yahweh put a mark on Cain's forehead so that no-one who found him would harm him. And Cain went out from Yahweh's presence and went to the Land of Nodh (= the land of wandering) which is to the east of Eden.

Imagine

Although they had been expelled from the garden, the Voice was not silent. Jahweh God, whose Voice it was, continued to seek them out in the cool of the evening – Red, Mother of Life, Produce and Mist. As the boys grew older, it became clear that the strange name

"Mother of Life had given her eldest son was remarkably appropriate. Produce" became skilled at farming. He loved growing things. He learned how to plant and prune and protect his plants so that they produced a good harvest. "Mist", on the other hand, developed a similar skill with animals. They responded to the gentleness of his touch as well as the food he bribed them with. He started to keep herds of goats and sheep and cows.

Jahweh God trained the two sons in a principle that many centuries later he would turn into law for the Israelites. He trained them to bring the first and the tenth of everything to him, the animals that were born to Mist's herds and the produce that Produce grew in his fields.

One year there was a particularly good harvest. Produce brought a selection of the early fruit and grain and presented it to Jahweh.

"It's not good enough." Produce heard as he stood in front of the altar piled with fruit, vegetables and grain.

"I can see into your heart," Jahweh continued. "You are giving reluctantly, resenting the fact that you have to hand it over to me. I know you haven't brought the best. This isn't the whole of the firstfruits, it's only some of it and I know that you've kept the best for yourself."

Produce scowled. His face flushed with a mixture of shame and resentment.

"Why are you angry?" Jahweh said. "If you do well, you'll be accepted. But if you don't, watch out, the sin demon is crouching at your door. It wants to possess you but you have to resist."

As Jahweh was uttering the words, Mist arrived, carrying a pile of

The first murder 41

> **Information**
> **The Land of Nod**
>
> The Hebrew word for "wandering" is "Nod". There is still an area on the West coast of the Caspian Sea that is known as Nodh to this day. What Cain ("Produce") did was terrible and wrong. But perhaps in time he produced what Paul later called the "fruits of repentance". God put a stop to his farming. But he developed other skills. He eventually became a town planner and builder. He found a wife and had a son called Enoch. And, at the time that Enoch was born, Cain was building the world's first city. With pride, he named it after his son.
>
> People who do terrible things have to face the consequences – those that come from God's justice and those that come from other people's reactions, which may not always be godly. Cain lost precious things through his rebellion and foolishness. But it wasn't the end of the story. God was still there for him. When we are repentant, God has new gifts to give, new things to teach us and new adventures waiting. Like Cain, each one of us can build a city on the ruins of our failure.

meat. Legs of lamb, joints of beef, Pork chops, rashers of bacon, whole chickens and turkeys. He piled them up on his altar alongside the altar Produce had built.

"Well done, Mist," the Voice of Jahweh spoke. "You've given nothing but the best."

Throughout the night Jahweh's words burned into Produce's heart. Resentment and anger grew. In the morning he asked his brother,

"It's going to be a big job to get in the rest of the harvest. Could you

Information
Who did Cain marry?

Who did Cain marry? The solution could lie in Genesis 5 v 4, which says "After Seth was born Adam lived 800 years and had other sons and daughters." The most obvious explanation is that Cain, and later his younger brother Seth, each married one of their sisters.

However, there is a problem with this solution in that the law of Moses forbids sexual relations between brother and sister. Arguably, the first generation status of Adam's children creates an exception to the rule.

The other possibility is that Adam wasn't necessarily the first or only human being created, just a special one. Some people see Genesis 1 v 26 as the creation of the human race in general and then Genesis 2 v 7 as the separate creation of a special man to inhabit the garden. In this case there would have been other humans around and both Cain and Seth could have chosen wives from these groups.

New Testament Links

There are references to Cain and Abel in
Hebrews 11 v 4
1 John 3 v 12
Jude 1 v 11

come to the fields and give me a hand?"

Innocently, Mist walked with his brother. He was bending down, cutting a plant, when Produce stepped behind him with a rock raised over his head. Years of feeling that his baby brother was the favourite, years of being told to be kind to him and look after him came to a head. The rock hit his skull with a crunching sound. Mist keeled over and a pool of blood began to form around his now lifeless head.

In the cool of the evening, Produce tried again. He'd brought a better offering this time. But Jahweh seemed not to notice.

'Where's Mist?" he said.

"I don't know," Produce snapped. "Am I my brother's herdsman?"

"What have you done, Produce?" Jahweh spoke. The voice was gentle, loving and compassionate, without a trace of anger. "Your brother's blood is crying to me from the ground. Now I'm going to have to curse you. I'm going to withdraw my anointing for farming. The land will no longer produce anything for you. You'll become a nomad, you'll have to hunt and scavenge for what food you can find. You'll be a rootless runaway."

The stress and guilt erupted into tears. "My punishment is more than I can bear!" Produce cried. "Whoever finds me is going to want to kill me."

"Not so." The Voice said. "If anyone kills Produce, he will suffer vengeance seven times over. I'm putting my mark on you so everyone will recognise you."

Chapter 5

The first city
The written account of Adam's Line (Part 4)

Scripture (Genesis 4 v 17–24)

And Cain had sex with his wife, she became pregnant and gave birth to Enoch. Cain was building a city and named it Enoch, after his son. Enoch had a son, Mehujael. Mehujael fathered Methushael and Methushael fathered Lamech.

Lamech took two wives, the name of the first was Adah and the name of the second was Zillah. Adah gave birth to Jabal. He was the father of people who live in tents and raise livestock. His brother's name was Jubal. He was the father of everyone who plays stringed and woodwind instruments. Zillah also gave birth, to Tubal Cain. He forged all kinds of tools out of bronze and iron. He had a sister, called Pleasant.

Lamech said to his wives, Adah and Zillah,

> "Listen to my voice, wives of Lamech
> Pay attention to what I'm saying.
> I have killed a man who injured me,
> A young man for wounding me.
> If sevenfold vengeance came on Cain
> For Lamech it will come seventy-sevenfold."

Imagine

The lamp flickered, making the shadows dance on the wall. Two women sat at the table in a fine, brick-built house in the city of Enoch.

One of them broke the anxious silence.

"It's late, Zillah. He should have been back a couple of hours ago. What can have kept him?"

"Adah, Let's pray to Jahweh that he is safe," Zillah replied.

They spoke in whispers, not wishing to disturb the four children who slept in an adjacent room.

Once, Adah and Zillah had been rivals. From the time they were children, whatever one had wanted the other had wanted too. They had squabbled and fought, even tore each other's hair out at times. The squabbling over possessions and the rivalry to be the dominant figure in their childhood games came to a focus when, as young women, they both fell in love with the same man, Lamech. They'd each used every feminine wile and manipulative deceit they could muster to win his affections, each determined that she was going to be the one he would choose. He had succumbed to both their charms – but not in the way either of them hoped for.

"There is no way I can choose between you," he had said. "If I pick one I will disappoint the other. I don't want to make either of you bitter. So I'll give you a choice. Either I marry both of you and you live with me together in peace. Or I reject you both and marry someone else."

"But no-one has ever married two women before," they said.

The first city

"There's a first time for everything," he said. "If I am faithful to the two of you and you are both faithful to me, what's the problem? I'll try to treat you equally and to love each of you the same. Many men will be envious of me for having a double blessing."

After a lot of discussion and argument, the two young women agreed.

"But no-one has ever married two women." Their relatives and neighbours said.

"There's a first time for everything." They replied.

The rivalry didn't end. They each tried hard to be Lamech's favourite. He worked hard to treat them both the same. In time, as they worked at it, they learned to get along together. Lamech smiled, inwardly, the first time they ganged up on him. It was good to see them setting aside the rivalry, even though it was at his expense.

They had each given birth to two children. Adah had two boys, Jabal and Jubal. Jabal loved animals and loved running about in the open air. Jubal was more studious. He was fascinated by music. He was always humming or whistling or banging out rhythms on anything that came to hand. Zillah had a boy and a girl. The boy, Tubal-Cain, was always doing things with his hands – digging or tying bits of wood together with wool or twine. He was fascinated by fire and would spend ages at the fireside, playing with the coals, watching how things burned. His sister, Pleasant, was still a baby.

Tonight, there was no rivalry. The two women were united in their anxiety and concern for their husband who should have been home hours before.

At last, they heard a noise outside the door. The door creaked on its hinges and Lamech stood in the doorway, his face covered in dried blood. There was a blood stain on his shirt. They both gasped as they looked at him.

"I was attacked." He explained.

Adah fetched a bowl and filled it with water. Zillah sorted out some old, clean material to use as bandages and towels. They set about cleaning his wounds. He explained how he had been set upon as he came back from the market place.

"They didn't take anything." He said. "I fought back. I wasn't going to let them take what I'd worked hard to get. But listen to me Adah, listen Zillah. There's something worse. We shall have to leave the city of Enoch and find somewhere else to live. I killed one of the young men who attacked me. I have blood on my hands. His family will want vengeance. We have to get together as much as we can carry and get out of here before they come after me. I'm guilty of bloodshed, like our ancestor, Cain. If God gave a sevenfold vengeance on anyone who killed Cain, I'll receive seventy sevenfold for for what I've done.

Then, in the early hours of the morning, before the sun rose, the unusual family of three adults and four children left the city of Enoch, the city Cain had built and named after his son. For four generations, Lamech's family had lived there, his father Methushael, his grandfather Mehujael, his great grandfather Irad and his great-great grandfather Enoch, the son of Cain. The curse of Cain had stayed in the family, lying dormant to the fourth generation and emerging again in Lamech. Now Lamech was going to have to start again from scratch just as Cain had done. What would happen to them?

Information

Later in the Bible it says that God allows the effects of sin to work its way through to the fourth generation. You can see the principle at work here. Cain shed blood and killed his brother. Four generations later, in Lamech, bloodshed and murder rear their ugly heads again. In our day we see the same curse still spreading its tentacles through the whole human race. To some degree at least, repentance and trust in Jesus' death on the cross can negate this generational effect of sin.

The streak of cunning that Eve and Adam introduced into the human race must have played a part in bringing about the polygamous relationship between Lamech and his two wives. Was the cunning on his part? Or their's? Or both?

The imagine section guesses that Lamech and his family would have had to flee from the city of Enoch, though this isn't stated in the Bible. Lamech's children appparently did well for themselves, though. The pioneering spirit that grew from the wanderings of Cain was in Lamech's children and at least four of them became pioneers.

Jabal was the world's first nomadic herdsman, earning a fortune from his flocks. Jubal became the world's first musician, the inventor of the harp and flute. Tubal-Cain, who loved playing with fire, discovered how to melt and mould metal and became the first blacksmith and maker of tools and weapons.

And little Naamah, whose name means "Pleasant"? We can guess that she married and had children, but the documents say no more about her.

Scripture
(Genesis 4 v 25 –26)

And Adam had sex with his wife and she gave birth to a son, whom she named Seth ("gift") because she said, "God has given me another offspring to replace Abel, whom Cain killed." He in turn had a son and called him Enosh. At that time people began to use the name Jaweh when they prayed.

Chapter 6

The first man dies
The written account of Adam's Line
(Part 4)

Scripture
When the scribe who first wrote Genesis 5 v 3–32 started making his marks on his clay tablet, no-one had thought of putting information in tabular form. If someone cooould have shown him how, I am sure he would have put this passage into a table. We are used to tables today, so that's how I have presented it – please see the next page.

Information – Cain's descendants and Seth's descendants

Genesis 4 listed the descendants of Cain and Genesis 5 lists the descendants of Seth. There are some names that occur in both lists. As far as I know, the solution I have suggested is a new one – that, as a sign of reconciliation, some of the descendants of Seth named their children after descendants of Cain. I have no evidence for it. It's just an idea, based on a hunch that Eve would have eventually longed to see Cain again and that, having built a city and had a son, he would have wanted his parents to enjoy his success with him.

The descendants of Adam. (Genesis 5 v 3–32)

When God created Adam he made him in the likeness of God. When he created them he made them male and female and he blessed them and called them both "mankind". When Adam had lived for 130 years he had a son who was like him in character and appearance and he gave him the name "Seth". After the birth of Seth, Adam lived another 800 years and fathered sons and daughters. The total life span of Adam was 930 years. Then he died.

Name	First son	Age at birth of first son	Other offspring	Rest of life (years)	Total life span (years)
Seth	Enosh	105	Other sons and daughters	807	912
Enosh	Kenan	90	Other sons and daughters	815	905
Kenan	Mahalel	70	Other sons and daughters	840	910
Mahalel	Jared	65	Other sons and daughters	830	895
Jared	Enoch[a]	162	Other sons and daughters	800	962
Enoch[a]	Methusaleh	65	Other sons and daughters	300[a]	365[a]
Methusaleh	Lamech	187	Other sons and daughters	782	969
Lamech[b]	Noah[c]	182	Other sons and daughters	595	777

[a] Enoch walked with God and then was no more because God took him.
[b] Lamech lived 182 years and bore a son and named him Noah. He said "He's going to comfort us after all the hard work and painful effort caused by the land Yahweh has cursed."
[c] After Noah was 500 years old he fathered Shem, Ham and Japheth.

The first man dies

Information

The ages in Genesis 5 and 11

Did people really live as long as they are supposed to have done according to the lists in Genesis 5 and Genesis 11? People have sought to explain these enormous ages in a number of ways. Simplifying the complex arguments, there are three possible explanations:

1. People did live to the ages that are recorded. This might have been because, in those days, there was less pollution and disease, the air was purer, their diet was better and they had less stress. Or it could simply be that God allowed people to live longer.

2. Some academics have suggested that the names listed are names of tribes. Each tribe is named after its founding head and in each case the "age" is the length of time that the tribe survived as a political unit rather than the actual age of the head.

3. Behind the word "year" in the Hebrew Bible there might lie a misunderstanding or mistranslation. For example, the original version of the story may have used a word that meant a season or a quarter of a year and this might have been translated wrongly as a year. If you divide the ages by 4 or 6 they become more believable. It could also be that the culture in which the ages were originally recorded did arithmetic in a different way to ours (for example using sixes the way we use tens). Again, it would then be easy for a translator to make a mistake.

These are plausible explanations but there is no evidence to support any of them.

Imagine

Mother of Life woke up. It was still dark but, through the window, the light of the dawn was beginning to break. She sensed that something was wrong. She sat up and, with one hand, brushed the long, white hair from her wrinkled face. The room was silent. It was a silence that filled her with fear. She turned to waken Red. She could dimly see the shape of his body lying beside her. She touched his shoulder. It was cold. She shook him. There was no response. With horror, she realised that the constant rhythm of his breathing had stopped. She screamed.

She knew, in the pit of her stomach, that the thing she dreaded the most had happened. It had been many, many years in the coming. But now the moment had arrived.

She felt it was her fault. They'd talked about it often, wondered what this day would be like. They'd known it had to come. "You must not blame yourself," he always said, "I had a choice. I could have said 'No.' I could have been taking better care of you." No matter what he said, she couldn't get away from the fact that she had given him the fruit that brought the death that now, finally, had come to him.

Information

The death of Adam

In 2008, two precious old men died who were the last surviving soldiers to have fought in the Great War. Their passing was of huge interest, marking the end of an era. How much more significant must have been the death of someone known, or believed, to have been the first person created by God? The Bible says nothing about how Adam died or how his death was commemorated. It doesn't even tell us whether Eve or Adam died first. I've taken a guess that Eve outlived him and that the words of the curse "your desire shall be for your husband", were partly fulfilled in her grief as a widow.

The first man dies

A day or two later, Mother of Life gathered with her sons and their sons and their son's sons, standing around the grave as Red's lifeless body was lowered into the ground. "Dust you are and to dust you shall return." Mother of Life remembered what God had said. Now it had happened. Cain, her firstborn "Produce", put his arm around her shoulder. She leaned her white head on his chest. It had been hard to forgive Cain for what he did to Abel. But he also was her son and she couldn't remain angry with him forever. She remembered the day so, so long ago, when Enoch arrived at their camp and said "I'm your grandson." He had told them about his father's city and taken them there to visit. Cain had invited them to come and live there with him.

Cain had been thrilled to discover he had a second brother and anxious to make up for what he had done by being a good brother to him. In time, several of Seth's offspring had sealed the reconciliation by naming their children after one or another of Cain's descendants. Seth's son, Enosh, started it by naming his son Kenan after Cain, as a sign of reconciliation. It had had a powerful spiritual effect that they had not expected. God, who had seemed distant and silent, suddenly began to talk to them again and the whole family had begun to worship him in the cool of the evening as she and her husband had done at the beginning.

Later Mahalel named his son Jared after Enoch's son Irad, and Jared then named his son Enoch. The second Enoch was special. He had been one of Mother of Life's favourites. He was so close to Jahweh that he spoke to him as he walked along, like you would with a friend. Until the day he disappeared. No-one ever found a body. They assumed God had just taken him away. Most recently there was Lamech, the youngest of the clan, named after the first Lamech who had run from the city after committing murder. Methuselah decided they must forgive him too. "Young" Enoch had told him God would reward his grace by giving him long life.

The day of Red's funeral was sad and stressful. To see Red laid in the earth was the harvest of the fruit that Mother of Life had eaten and given him to eat. For a while she would experience the loneliness Red had known in the garden before God gave her to him. Soon it would be her turn to die. She was comforted by her huge family. So many wonderful men and women who had sprung from her womb. Jahweh had been merciful to her. It wasn't long before there was a new addition to the family.

"Come on dear, another push should do it! Nearly over!"

The midwife eased the slippery, blood-covered bundle from between the mother's legs, wiped it all over and gave it a little tap on the back. It gasped for breath and then began to emit a complaining cry.

"Here you are. You have a son."

"Hello, little one!" The baby's mother took the bundle from the midwife's arms and gazed adoringly at her little boy. Lamech, his father, stepped forward from the corner of the room and bent over the bed to look. Something came welling up inside him, a hope, a certainty, even, that this child was going to make a difference to the world they lived in.

We'll call him "Comfort", he said. "He's going to comfort us after all the labour and painful toil of our hands caused by the ground the Lord has cursed."

New Testament Link

Jude refers to Enoch in Jude 1 v 14.

Chapter 7

The first superheroes
The account of Noah (part 1)

Scripture (Genesis 6 v 1–8)

When Adam's descendants increased on the earth and daughters were born to them, the sons of God saw that the daughters of Adam were beautiful and took as wives any of them they chose. Yahweh said, "My spirit will not strive within man forever. His flesh will be mortal and his maximum life span will be 120 years." The Nephilim were in the earth in those days – and also later on. The sons of God used to go in to the daughters of Adam and have children by them, which were the famous valiant warriors of olden times.

But God saw that the wickedness of mankind was great in the earth and his thoughts were inclined to evil all day long. He regretted that he had made humankind in the earth and his heart was filled with pain. Yahweh said, "I am going to wipe out humankind whom I have created and clear them from the surface of the ground, along with the animals and reptiles and birds. I have changed my mind about making them."

But Jahweh liked Noah.

Imagine

A millennium and a half had passed since God first breathed the breath of life into Adam. Originally there had been several kinds of human beings. Some counted their origin from the moment when God said "Let us make man in our image." They called themselves "the children of God".

Adam's descendants regarded themselves as special and separate from the other human beings because God had individually formed Adam and breathed into his nostrils the breath of life. Other humans might call themselves "children of God" but they didn't know Jahweh God the way Adam's descendants did. It was only Adam's descendants who walked with God and heard his voice. True, Adam had rebelled against God by eating the forbidden fruit. But that didn't change the fact that he had been created separately to all the others. So the descendants of Adam had kept themselves apart – to begin with, at least.

The separation was in part to protect their special relationship with Jahweh God. But they were aware that they also needed to protect the rest of mankind from the dreadful effects of Adam and Eve's disobedience. By eating the "forbidden fruit", "Red" and "Life Mother" had brought something dangerous into the world. It wasn't just that they were under a curse. They were infected with a bias towards deceit and cunning.

Originally, the various groups lived in different parts of the earth with no need to meet. But as they multiplied, they spread out and filled the earth with farms and villages and towns and cities. In time, the different races of human beings met and began to interact. Some of Adam's descendants were still careful to keep themselves separate. There was a clean line, for example, all the way from Seth to

Methuselah's son, Lamech. But it wasn't the case with all their relatives.

The descendants of Adam were especially good looking. The genes that Eve passed down produced some amazingly beautiful women as well as handsome sons. Adam's offspring were increasingly under pressure from the children of God to intermarry with them. Men from among the children of God were willing to pay huge dowries for the privilege of marrying a daughter of Adam. Some were less scrupulous and took what they wanted by force, kidnapping and raping daughters of Adam when they could catch them on their own and unprotected.

The mixing of the different gene pools produced some amazing offspring – men and women with incredible strength or extreme intelligence. But, as different branches of the human race mixed and mingled, the distinctions between them were gradually erased. The effects of the curse began to be spread through the whole human race. All of them carried the tendency to cunning. The cunning spread and showed itself in so many ways – in theft, in embezzlement, in rape, in adultery, in murder and violence, in deceit and trickery.

God couldn't let it go on unchecked. He couldn't leave the victims unavenged. He had to do something.

"Comfort" (Noah, in Hebrew) was part of his plan.

Information

Genesis 6 verses 1–8 is one of the most intriguing passages in the Bible. Who are the "sons of God" and the "daughters of men"? Why is their interbreeding frowned on and why does it result in superhero offspring? There are no clear answers – only suggestions (which I'm going to add to). The various experts who have tried to make sense of it have come up with three theories. I've added a fourth. I've never heard this one from anyone else but I think it has something going for it.

Theory 1 – angelic beings
According to this theory the "sons of God" are angels who take on human form in order to have sex with human women. The offspring of these pairings have superhuman powers. On this view the angels who acted in this way disobeyed God and, consequently, are now imprisoned in darkness awaiting judgement (see Jude verse 6). This is the traditional Christian view and was common in the early centuries of church history. It is not without problems, though. Jesus' teaching implies that angels are not sexual (Mark 12 v 25). And when were they consigned to darkness? Immediately after sinning, or later? If later, when?

Theory 2 – Seth's offspring
This view is more recent. According to this theory, the sons of God are Seth's offspring and the daughters of Adam are women descended from Cain. A problem with this view is that the description "daughters of Adam" could apply equally to women descended from Seth or from Cain.

Theory 3 – nobility
In this view the term "sons of God" was applied to rulers, the nobility. The "daughters of Adam" were girls from ordinary families. This view has been commonly held among Jewish commentators.

Theory 4 (my theory) – more than one kind of human being.
There were two kinds of human being, created in different ways. One group were created by God's command and are referred to in Genesis 1 verses 26–30. They are described as created in God's image and hence are called "children of God" ("son of" in Hebrew can mean "like"). Adam was thus not the first human being but a new man, specially created, separate to the other humans. He alone was shaped by God from dust and received the breath of life. The "daughters of Adam" are women descended from Adam and Eve. This passage records the beginning of interbreeding between these two groups.

All four of these explanations run up against the problem that the Nephilim are also mentioned later in the Bible in Numbers 13 v 33. They thus appear both before and after the flood. It could be that the name "Nephilim" was separately applied to two different sets of people, one before the flood and one after. Perhaps the post-flood Nephilim were given the name as a nickname because they were like the legendary Nephilim of old. Another possibility is that one or more of Noah's daughters in law had Nephilim among her ancestors and carried recessive Nephilim genes which resulted in the emergence of extra large and extra strong offspring further along the family line.

Chapter 8

The first ocean voyage
The account of Noah (Part 2)

Scripture (Genesis 6 v 9–7 v 24)

Noah always did what was right. In his lifetime he was blameless. Noah walked with God. He had three sons, Shem, Ham and Japheth.

The earth was corrupt in God's eyes and full of proud aggression. God examined the earth. It had become rotten because every human being on earth had corrupted their ways. So God said to Noah,

"I'm going to cut off every human being since the earth is full of aggression because of them. I am going to cut them off and the earth with them. So, make yourself a container constructed from coated wood. Make rooms in it and coat it with bitumen inside and out. This is how you are to construct it. The container must be 137 metres long, 23 metres wide and 14 metres high. Make a roof for it and finish the container with a roof overhang of 457 mm. Put a door in the side and make lower, middle and upper decks. I am going to bring floods of water on the earth to drown every living thing that is on the earth and under the heavens. But I am going to establish my covenant with you. You will go into the container, you and your sons and your wife and your sons' wives with you. You must bring into the container two of every living creature, male and female, to keep them alive with you – two of every kind of bird, of every kind of animal and every kind of creature that moves across the ground. They will come to you to be kept alive. You are to take every kind of food that is to be eaten and store it away as food for you and for them."

And Noah did everything God told him. Whatever God told him, he did. Then Yahweh said to Noah,

"Go, you and all your household, into the container, because I have observed that you are behaving in the right way in the sight of this generation. Of each of the ritually clean beasts, take with you seven males and seven females and of the unclean beasts take one male and one female, to keep their various species alive all over the earth. In seven days' time I am going to send rain on the earth for forty days and forty nights and I am going to wipe away everything I have made from the surface of the ground."

And Noah did exactly as Jahweh instructed him. Noah was 600 years old when the waters flooded the earth and Noah, his sons, his wife and the wives of his sons went into the container that floated on the surface of the flood waters. Clean animals and unclean animals, birds and everything that crawls along the ground came to Noah, two by two, male and female, to the container, just as Yahweh had commanded him. And on the seventh day the flood waters came on the earth. In the six hundredth year of Noah's life, on the seventeenth day of the second month – that was the day when all the springs of the great deep opened up and the floodgates in the skies were opened and rain fell on the earth for forty days and forty nights. On that exact day Noah went into the container with his sons, with Shem and Ham and Japheth, and with his wife and the wives of his three sons, with every form of wild animal and every form of livestock, every form of life that moves across the ground, every kind of bird and everything with wings. Every kind of living being came to Noah in pairs to enter the ark. A male and a female of every living being came as God had instructed Noah. Then Jahweh shut him in.

The floods kept coming on the earth for 40 days. The waters increased greatly over the earth and the container floated on the surface of the water. The waters rose higher and higher above the earth and all the famous hills everywhere under the heavens were covered. The waters rose fifteen cubits above the tops of the hills.

Everything on the earth that was alive died; all the livestock, all the wild animals, everything that crawls on the earth and all the people. Everything on the ground that breathed the spirit of life in its nostrils died. Every living thing was wiped from the surface of the earth – people and animals and things that crawl along the ground and birds of the air. They were all wiped off the face of the earth. Only Noah remained and those with him in the ark. The water flooded the earth for 150 days.

Imagine

"Hi Shem! Great to see you, mate, how're doing?" Ham clapped his brother on his back. Japheth reached out his hand in greeting.

"Sorry I'm late." Shem said, "I got held up on the way, giving some help to someone who had been mugged and robbed. This neighbourhood just seems to get worse. Any idea what this meeting's all about?"

"No idea at all," said Japheth. 'Dad was pretty insistent that we come together, so it must be important."

Their mother came in with a plate of food, quickly put it down and gave Shem a warm hug. Noah was behind her. He greeted the three young men and encouraged his wife out of the room, closing the door behind her.

"OK lads, you'll be wondering why I've called you together. Well. I need your help with a really big project. It's too much for me on my own but I have to do it. It's a matter of life and death for us all. It's got to be done."

"Just tell us what you want to do Pops. For you, we'll do anything. Well, anything within reason", Japheth interjected, confidently.

"When you hear what I'm planning, you may think it's not within reason, Noah replied. " I want to build a boat."

"No problem," said Ham. "I've built boats before. We can harvest the reeds from the river nearby."

"No, not a little reed boat," Noah responded. "It's not like any boat you've ever seen before. Thing is, I've had a warning from God. There's going to be a huge flood. The whole of the world, or at least the part we know about, it's all going to be buried under several feet of water.

Information

Stories of a man rescuing his family and animals in a boat are found in nearly every culture in the world, including native tribes in both North and South America. There are several versions of the story in the middle east. The later Sumerians knew Noah as Ziusudra (Meaning "the far distant long lived one"). To the Semitic speaking peoples of early Mesopotamia he was Atrahasis ("the exceedingly devout one"). The later Mesopotamians knew him as Utnapishtim. The "na" part of this name is probably the same as the name the Bible gives him, "Noah".

The first ocean voyage

Nothing is going to survive, unless it can float. God's had enough of the violence and treachery of the human race and he's going to destroy them all, except us. He wants us to build a big boat. He wants us to build it out of gopher wood and to make it waterproof by coating it with bitumen. Come and look at the plans."

Noah took them to an outbuilding where he had fixed a mosaic of clay tiles to a wall, showing a diagram of the floating box he was planning. The three men gathered round to look.

Shem whistled with amazement. "You've got to be joking Dad!" said Ham. "It's enormous!" agreed Japheth.

"I'm not joking," said Noah. We're talking about a floating container 137 metres long, 23 metres wide and 14 metres high, with three decks. You see, it's not only going to take us and our families, it's also going to take a pair of every kind of animal, and provisions for a long time. God seems to be telling me that the rains will last 40 days and 40 nights and all the vegetation is going to be destroyed. It will be a year at least before the earth recovers.

There was a long silence. Then,

"Are you sure about this?" said Shem.
"Positively sure," said Noah.
"We don't have a choice then, do we?" Shem continued.
"When do we start?" Japheth chipped in.

They started the next day. Gradually, over a period of 18 months, the construction took shape. When the neighbours began to see the top deck rising above the treeline, Noah's container became a tourist attraction. People came from miles away to marvel, to ask questions, to laugh and poke fun at the sheer craziness of the plan.

Once the container had been built and coated with bitumen, they faced the task of capturing and herding the animals and gathering the supplies, both for the animals and for themselves. That process again took several months. They took into the ark one pair of every

Information

What caused the flood?

David Rohl, a biblical archaeologist, in his book *The Lost Testament,* describes a convincing natural explanation for the flood, which he places in the year 3114 BC. According to his theory, at that time the whole planet was suffering from a global climate change caused by a major volcanic eruption in the Aleutian Islands. Millions of tons of ash and sulphuric acid had been belched into the atmosphere, blotting out sunlight and causing a mini ice age with severe winters and cool summers. Normally, in the mountains to the north of the Mesopotamian plain, the snow would melt during the summer, flooding the Tigris and Euphrates rivers. But for five years the snow, thicker than usual in the winter, failed to melt in the summer and simply accumulated.
Then, one spring, the thaw came. Five years of accumulated snow melted and flooded down from the mountains, swelling the rivers. At the same time the thick layer of sulphuric acid crystals that had accumulated in the atmosphere began to dissolve and fall to earth as torrential rain. Strong south winds drove up the Persian Gulf, causing a further rise in sea levels. As a result the whole of the Mesopotamian plain was flooded in a major disaster that swept away a whole civilisation.

However, Francis Schaeffer argued that the flood must have been prior to 20,000 BC becase anthropologists date the entry of American Indians into America via the Bering Straits at this time and the American Indians were descendants of Noah.

kind of unclean animal, seven of each kind of clean animal (those they used for sacrifice or were allowed to eat) and seven of each kind of bird. The time came when everything was ready. The ark was finished and stocked with provisions. The animals had been gathered, not in the ark yet but in pens nearby, ready to be taken in. Noah reported to God "Lord, the ark is ready."

"I know," said God. You have one week to get your family and all the animals into the ark."

"Let's have a trial run," Noah said to his family. They moved in all the animals, the grandchildren, Noah's daughters in law, the three sons. Noah pulled the door shut.

"That's good, well done," he said. "Once the rain starts, we'll be ready. OK, everyone out again."

He pushed at the door. It was stuck.

"I don't understand!" he said. "It opened and shut perfectly well before."

"Noah, what have you done?" his wife asked, accusingly.

"Nothing," he said. "But I can't open the door. It's as if someone is holding it shut from the other side."

At that moment, they heard the drumming of the raindrops on the roof. It continued for days. After several days, they heard a grinding and creaking noise deep in the base of the vessel and the deck began to move underneath them.

"It's floating!" Shem exclaimed.

Information

How extensive was the flood?

David Rohl's scenario sees the flooding of the Mesopotamian plains in 3114 BC as being the same as Noah's flood. Francis Schaeffer argued for a much earlier date and a truly universal flood. Which is right? To be honest no-one can be certain. In David Rohl's scenario the flood is widespread but it didn't cover the earth entirely. Because of this Christians who want to be faithful to the Bible tend to go with Francis Schaeffer and look for a situation where the whole of the planet was covered with water. Genesis 7 verse 19 is a key part of the discussion. The Authorised King James Version translated this as:

> "the waters prevailed exceedingly on the earth and all the high hills that were under the whole heaven were covered."

This seems to imply that the whole planet was under water. However there is some leeway in the translation. The Hebrew word translated "earth" means the ground, not necessarily the planet, and the word translated "high hills" ("mountains" in the New International Version) was often applied to the mounds on which cities were built. So it is legitimate to translate this verse "the waters rose high above the ground and the all the city mounds under the whole heaven were covered."

In those days the population of the world would have been smaller and human habitations would have been largely grouped around rivers, lakes and seashores. Civilisation demanded ready access to water for drinking, bathing, fishing and transport. Even after the invention of the wheel, watercourses were vital routes for transporting heavy goods. Human habitations tended to hug the

The first ocean voyage

shorelines and rivers rather than clearing the thick inland forests or trying to tame the deserts and mountains. It would thus have been quite possible for the whole human race to be destroyed without every area of land being flooded.

Using the scenario David Rohl describes, the accumulation of snow on mountains would not have been restricted to the area that fed the waters of the Tigris and the Euphrates. The alps, the Himalayas, the Andes and the Rockies would all have had a similar accumulation of snow and these snows all melted in the same period. The excessive rains, too would have been a worldwide phenomenon. Perhaps tsunamis were also part of the picture. So David Rohl's suggestion can fit the Biblical evidence – but we can't be certain.

Scripture (Genesis 8 v 1– 19)

But God kept in mind Noah and all the wild animals and livestock that were with him in the container and he sent a wind over the earth and the waters receded. The springs of the deep and the floodgates of the heavens had been closed and the rain had stopped falling from the sky. The water kept withdrawing from the ground. After 150 days the water had gone down and the container came to rest on the mountains of Urarat. The waters kept going down until the tenth month and on the first day of the tenth month you could see the tops of the hills.

After another 40 days, Noah opened the window that he had made in the container. He sent out a raven which kept flying out in vain until the water had dried up from the ground. Then he also sent out a pigeon to find out if the waters had dried up from the surface of the ground. But the pigeon could find nowhere to land and it returned to Noah in the container because there was water over the entire surface of the earth. Noah put out his hand and caught the pigeon and brought it back into the container. He waited another seven days and then sent the pigeon from the container again. The pigeon came back to him in the evening and in its beak it had a freshly plucked olive leaf – so then Noah knew that the water was receding from the land. He waited another week and then released the pigeon again but this time it didn't come back to him. By the first day of the first month of Noah's 601st year, the water had dried up from the earth. Noah removed the shell of the container and saw that the surface of the ground was dry. By the 27th day of the second month the earth was completely dry.

Then God spoke to Noah and said, "Come out of the container, you, your wife, your sons and your son's wives. And bring out every living thing that is with you, the birds, the animals, the creatures that move along the ground, so that they can be fruitful and multiply all over it."

And Noah came out with his sons and his wife and his son's wives. All the animals and all the creatures that crawl along the ground and all the birds, everything that moves on the earth, they all came out of the ark, one species at a time.

Imagine

For almost five weeks the rain continued to beat on the roof of the ark. The vessel pitched and tossed. Huge waves lifted it up and then dropped it. At times it was like being in an elevator that kept shooting up and down between floors with the doors never opening. At other

The first ocean voyage

times it was like being rocked from side to side in the darkness. The wooden structure creaked and groaned but held together and, more importantly, stayed watertight. A terrible stench began to fill the boat as urine and faeces accumulated in the bottom level. Fortunately, because the smell developed gradually, the humans living on the top deck were accustomed to it. Every now and then, there were periods of calm when the motion became more stable. At these times it was possible to light oil lamps to help them see in the darkness and to busy themselves with chores, such as rationing out the clean water, mucking out the animal pens and cages or even cooking food.

At the end of five weeks a change came about. The noise of the rain stopped. They still could hear the wind whistling around the structure of the container, the noises of the animals below and the slapping of the waves against the sides. But the constant background hiss of the rain was no longer there.

In the darkness within the container it was difficult to calculate the passage of time. The menstrual cycle of the women was the only clock they had. The women had been through their cycle five times.

Then one day, suddenly, a scraping and grinding sound vibrated through the whole of the boat. The beams creaked as if the whole vessel was complaining. And the constant motion stopped.

It was clear that the container was grounded. It was still surrounded by water but it was resting on something firm.

This new situation made things easier. Noah and his sons began to be concerned by the fact that supplies of fresh water and oil for the lamps were running low. And the hold at the bottom of the ark that took all the sewage was almost full. The rain had been stopped for a long time now and the ark continued to be motionless, so Noah made a hole in the side of their living quarters and fashioned it into a window that they could open and close. It was a relief to smell the fresh air, though it suddenly made them more aware of the putrid atmosphere inside the ark. As they looked out of the window, all they could see was water in every direction. They could see dolphins and whales leaping and splashing in the distance. Seabirds swooped and dived over shoals of fish or rested, bobbing up and down on the water. Now and then they could spot debris and the bloated corpses of people or animals floating on the surface. But there was no land. There were no other boats, no other people.

They waited another five weeks. Then Noah decided on an experiment. He took one of the ravens from its cage and released it. It flew around in a circle and came back to the ark. He repeated the experiment again each day for several days, with the same result. Then he tried the same experiment with a pigeon. The pigeon flew off

Information

A white dove carrying an olive branch in its mouth has become a universal symbol of peace and hope. This is where the symbol started. The dove family, of course, includes the homing pigeon and that's how I've chosen to imagine it.

The apostle Peter saw the ark as a picture of baptism. Noah and his family put their trust in what God had said and obediently built the ark. Their faith, expressed in the building of the ark, kept them safe through the waters of the flood. In a similar way, Christian disciples are saved from the flood of God's judgement by their faith expressed in baptism. In baptism they are overwhelmed with water but come up triumphant. In later Christian imagery, the ark also became an image of the church, which contains the faithful family of God's people and keeps them safe through the stormy seas of life in a godless world.

purposefully and disappeared over the horizon. Using her natural homing instinct, she was heading for where her home was – or where it had been. A day later, she returned. She had flown home, found there was nowhere to land and come back again. Noah held out his hand. The pigen hopped onto it and Noah took her back inside.

He waited another week and tried sending her out again. This time she came back, carrying in her beak a green olive twig with leaves on it. "The water is definitely going down. Somewhere there's some dry land with a tree on it!", Noah told his family.

Another week passed by and Noah sent the pigeon out once more. This time she didn't return. Noah took her mate and sent him off after her. He too, didn't come back. "They've found somewhere to feed and build a nest," he thought.

He leaned out of the window and looked down. The water level had now sunk below the bottom of the container, which was now stuck on a rocky island.

Day by day the water continued to recede. Other rocky peaks began to poke through the surface and gradually joined up until now all they could see was land. Now and then it rained again, but not how it had done before. The showers were gentle and came to an end as the clouds passed over. They were able to collect some much-needed fresh water. Eventually the land was dry enough for them to open up the door and let down the gangway. They were able to let out some of the insects and birds and to clear out some of the sewage.

They set about gathering stones which they used to build enclosures where they could pen the sheep and goats and cattle. Eventually they were able to release the wild animals, taking care to give the grass and leaf eating creatures a head start on the wild meat eaters.

Soon, they would be able to leave the container themselves and begin a new life.

Information

Where did the ark come to rest?

The account in Genesis says that the ark came to rest on the Mountains of Ararat. The plural, "mountains" is significant. From the time of the middle ages until recently, people have assumed that the ark came to rest on Mount Ararat in Eastern Turkey, near the border with Armenia. Various expeditions have visited the mountain trying to find evidence of the ark's presence there. However, an older tradition locates the ark's resting place as another mountain, now called called Judi Dagh. This location is much further south, in Kurdistan, 120 kilometres north of the town of Mosul. Judi Dagh is part of the Zagros mountain range. The area that includes both these mountains was once known as Urartu. Eutychius, the 9th century bishop of Alexandria, stated, "The ark rested on the mountains of Ararat, that is Gebel Judi, near Mosul."

This makes Judi Dagh a more likely site than Ararat. The Nestorian Christians in the 5th Century built monasteries on Judi Dagh to commemorate the grounding of the ark. According to a local tradition people used to collect fragments of bitumen from the remains of the ark and this practice continued as late as the 19th century. Bitumen occurs naturally in pools in many places in the Mesopotamian plain but does not occur naturally in the mountains.

Chapter 9

The first covenant
The account of Noah (Part 3)

Scripture (Genesis 8 v 20–9 v 17)

And Noah built an altar to Yahweh and sacrificed on it every kind of ritually clean animal and every kind of ritually clean bird. God smelt the pleasant aroma and said in his heart, "Never again will I curse the ground because of man, although his heart is biased to evil from childhood. And never again will I destroy every living creature.

"As long as earth remains,
Sowing time and reaping time,
Cold and heat,
Summer and winter,
Day and night,
Will not stop."

Then God blessed Noah and his sons. He said to them, "Be fruitful, multiply and fill the earth. All animals, all birds, everything that crawls on the ground and all the fish in the sea will be in fear and dread of you. I have given them all to you. Every living thing that moves will be food for you. I give you them all to eat, just as I gave you the green plants. But you must not eat flesh with blood in it. For in the blood is the breath of life. I will demand a repayment for any living thing and from each man for the life of his fellow man.

"Shed the blood of a person
By a person your blood shall be shed
For people are made in God's image."

As for you, be fruitful and multiply, increase in the earth and become many within it.

And God said to Noah and to his children,
"To you I am saying, 'I am making my covenant with you, with your children and with every living thing that is with you – the birds, the livestock and all the wild animals, all those who came out of the ark with you and every living thing on earth. I am establishing my covenant with you all that never again will every living thing be cut off by the waters of a flood and never again will there be a flood that swallows up the earth.

"This is the sign of the covenant I am making with you and every living thing associated with you. It is a covenant for all generations to come. I have set my rainbow in the clouds and it will be the sign of the covenant between me and the earth. Whenever I bring clouds over the earth and the rainbow appears in the clouds, I will remember my covenant between me and you and all living creatures of every species that never again will the waters of a flood swallow up everything that lives.

"Whenever the bow appears in the clouds I will look at it and remember the unending covenant between God and every living thing on earth of whatever species." And God said to Noah, "This is the symbol of the covenant that I am making with every living thing on the earth."

Imagine

There was a lot to do before they could finally leave the ark. They had to find a suitable location for new homes, not only for Noah and his wife but for Shem, Ham, Japheth and their wives and children too. Then they had to gather the materials they needed and set to work building their new homes.

After a trek through the mountain they found a place where the foothills met a large, fertile plain. The hillside was full of springs and they decided to move their belongings there. Noah picked a south-facing slope for his patch of land. There was something he particularly wanted to grow there and the location would be ideal. They built new pens for the domesticated animals and then went back to the ark to prepare to move all their belongings to the new location.

In the late afternoon, the day before they hoped to load up their belongings and move away from the ark, Noah built an altar and offered a sacrifice. The smoke from the fire on the altar drifted up into the sky. It was an emotion-filled moment. They remembered with horror and sadness what had happened, they felt intense gratitude to God for keeping them safe and a mixture of excitement and anxiety about what lay ahead.

They'd been standing with their faces towards the sun. Suddenly one of the children shouted,

"Look! Look! Over there!"

They all turned round to see a rainbow arching against the clouds in the sky to the east. Everyone gasped. "It's beautiful!"
"It's a sign from God," Noah said.

Information

Covenant

God gives the rainbow as a constant reminder of the covenant he makes with Noah and, through him, with the whole human race. A covenant is a binding promise – a bit like a contract but with an important difference. A contract involves two parties, both of which agree to abide by the terms of the agreement between them but, with a covenant, the promise is one-sided, "I bind myself legally to act in this way to you, irrespective of whether you make any similar promise to me." Christian marriage for example, is a covenant, not a contract, hence the words "for better for worse" used in some marriage ceremonies. It's not "we agree to do this so long as we both keep our promise" but each person saying "I agree to do this however you behave to me."

Covenants are central to God's interaction with human beings. In the course of history God made several covenants with mankind. The first was to provide mankind with food (see Genesis 1 v 29 – 30). The covenant with Noah is the second covenant. God goes on to make further covenants with Abraham (Genesis 15 and 17), with Jacob (Genesis 28), with Moses (Exodus 19 and 20), with Joshua (Joshua 1), David (1 Chronicles 17) and, finally the new covenant he has made with us through Jesus (see Jeremiah 31 v 33 Jeremiah 32 v 40 and 1 Corinthians 11 v 26).

When John the apostle provides a symbolic description of the throne of God in heaven in Revelation 4 v 3 he describes a rainbow around God's throne, a constant reminder of his covenant with the human race.

The first covenant

They stood, silently gazing at the rainbow and, as they gazed, a warm, comforting presence wrapped itself round them, as if an enormous Being was standing behind them gathering them into its arms.

It was a presence that Noah knew only too well. A presence that generations of his ancestors had also known, back through Methuselah and Enoch and Jared and Kenan and Seth, all the way to Adam himself who first met the Presence in the garden in the cool of the evening. Noah recognised the inner compulsion to listen. He heard the inner Voice and spoke out loud the words that formed in his heart,

"While the earth remains,
"Seedtime and harvest
Cold and heat
Summer and winter
Day and night
Will never cease…

"This is the sign of the covenant I am making with you for all generations to come…

"Never again will there be a flood to destroy the earth … "

New Testament Links

Noah is mentioned in the New Testament in:
Matthew 24 v 37, 38
Luke 17 v 26, 27
Hebrews 11 v 7
1 Peter 3 v 20
2 Peter 2 v 5

Chapter 10
The first drunk
The account of Shem, Ham and Japheth

Scripture (Genesis 9 v 18– 28)

The sons of Noah who came out of the container were Shem, Ham and Japheth. Ham was the father of Canaan. Noah had three sons and from them came the people scattered through the whole earth.

Noah was a man of the soil and he planted a vineyard. He drank some of the wine, got drunk and uncovered himself in his tent. Ham, Canaan's father, looked at his father's nakedness and reported it to his two brothers outside. Then Shem and Japheth took a garment and laid it across their shoulders. They walked in backwards and covered their father's nakedness. They turned their eyes away so as to not look at the nakedness of their father. When Noah woke from his drunken sleep, he learned what his youngest son had done to him. He said,

"A curse on Canaan!
May he forever be the lowest slave of his brothers,"

Then he said,
"May Jahweh bless Shem; may Canaan be his slave.

May Jahweh extend Japheth's territory;
May Japheth live in Shem's tents and may Canaan be his slave too."

After the flood, Noah lived for 350 years. The full extent of Noah's lifespan was 950 years. Then he died.

Imagine

There was so much to do. As well as tending the animals, they needed to clear fields and plant them with the store of seed they had brought into the ark, to ensure a good harvest.

They also needed to build permanent houses. To begin with, they lived in tents or temporary shelters. The building work was very much a spare time activity and proceeded quite slowly. Noah put the emphasis on building homes for the boys and their families first. He and his wife were still living in a tent after several years.

High on Noah's list of priorities was his vision for the south-facing slope he had earmarked for part of his personal estate. He had brought a collection of grape vines with him in the ark and, gradually, he began to build up a substantial vineyard. As he had thought, the south facing slope was an ideal setting for growing grapes.

He loved grapes. His vineyard became his pride and joy. As well as eating them, he found a way of pressing them so that he could gather and store the juice. After a few years he had a bumper crop. He filled scores of containers with the sweet drink and, unbeknown to him, some of them began to ferment.

When they finally moved into a house, he moved the tent to his vineyard and used it as a place where he could shelter from the heat of the day or the occasional rain shower. One day he'd been working

The fist drunk

hard and, as the sun rose high, he went to his tent to rest. He was thirsty and drank several litres of grape juice to quench his thirst. The taste was different, he couldn't work out why. But he was too thirsty to bother. He began to feel very happy and carefree. He took off his clothes because he was feeling so hot. And he kept having just a little more of the fermented juice.

Shem, Ham and Japheth were expecting Noah to join them in the afternoon but he didn't arrive. Normally, they could see him, moving around among his vines but he was nowhere to be seen. So they walked up the hillside to where he had pitched his tent.

As they climbed the slope, Ham and his young son Canaan, the youngest and fittest, went bounding up the hill ahead of the others. Japheth and Shem were a long way behind. Canaan and Ham reached the tent first. They went in and, as the others arrived, they came out, grinning and chuckling to themselves.

"Grandpa's got no clothes on!" Canaan said.

"Yes," Ham added. "He's lying there fast asleep as naked as the day he was born, flat on his back."

Canaan started to elaborate, "I could even see his ..."

But he stopped short as Ham clapped his hand over his son's face and said, "That's enough!"

"Have some respect for your father," Shem scolded.

Shem and Japheth discussed for a moment what they should do. They fetched a blanket and then walked backwards into the tent, holding the blanket between them and taking care not to look at their father. Only when they had covered his naked body did they try again to rouse him. Eventually they succeeded but, to begin with, he was disorientated and aggressive. Eventually he began to sober up. He was still slightly tipsy but began to put two and two together and to realise that there must have been something about the fermented grape juice that had affected him in this way. "It made me feel really happy to start with," he said, "And then I got confused and couldn't stand up and didn't know what I was doing."

"Well, thank you for covering me up, boys."

"Daddy and I saw you with no clothes on," said Canaan. Noah asked some questions and found out exactly what had happened. If he hadn't still been slightly under the influence of the wine, he might have thought twice about what he said next. Was it inspired by the Holy Spirit or was it just the wine talking? Either way, what he said next shaped history.

"Curse Canaan, may he be the lowest of slaves to his brothers
Bless the Lord, who is Shem's God
May Canaan's descendants be Shem's slaves
May God extend Japheth's territory
May Japheth live in Shem's tents
And may Canaan be his slave."

Information

People disagree as to whether any blame attaches to Noah in this incident. There are two ways of looking at it.

First view
This passage appears in the Bible to show that Noah was a sinner like everyone else. None of the heroes of faith was perfect. Jacob

was a cheat, Moses a murderer, David was an adulterer and Noah was a drunk. He over indulged knowing what he was doing. He was wrong to get drunk and lie about in a state of undress. He cursed his son and his grandson inappropriately while he was still under the influence of alcohol.

Second view
This passage apears in the Bible to explain the history of the descendants of Ham. The Bible describes Noah as "blameless" (Genesis 6 v 9). Noah discovered wine and its intoxicating effects by accident. His drunkenness and intoxicated behaviour were the result of ignorance. Ham found Noah in a state of undress and made fun of him to his brothers. There is even a hint in the wording of the original text that Ham may have sexually abused the old man. Cursing Ham and extending the curse to later generations of his family was an understandable response to a son who had dishonoured and possibly abused him when he was vulnerable.

The passage does not say whether Noah was right to issue the curse or not. It simply reports what Noah did and said. Later on some Canaanites (descended from Ham) became slaves to the Israelites, who were descendants of Shem, when they occupied the promised land. The editor who included this account in Genesis may have seen this as an outworking of Noah's curse. But the writer is merely reporting what he has heard and observed. Even if the fortunes of Ham and Canaan's descendants *were* influenced by Noah's curse, that does not mean that God himself approved of the curse or deliberately brought about its fulfilment.

Some of Ham's descendants eventually settled in Africa. In the past his has been used as a pretext for appalling racism.

Scripture (Genesis 10 v 2–7)

These are the clans of Noah's sons, according to their lines of descent, within their nations. From these the nations spread out over the earth after the flood.

The sons of Japheth	Gomer	Sons of Gomer	Ahskenaz Riphath Togarmah
	Magog		
	Madai		
	Javan	Sons of Javan*	Elishah Tarshish The Kittim The Rodanim*
	Tubal		
	Meshech		
	Tiras		

* From these the coastal people spread into their territories according to their clans within their nations, each with its own language.

The Sons of Ham by their clans and languages in their territories and nations			
Cush	Mizraim	Put	Canaan**
Seba Havilah Sabtah Raama Sabteca Nimrod*	Ludiites Anamites Lehabites Naphtuhites (from whom the Philistines came) Caphtorites		Sidon (his firstborn) Hittites Jebusites Amorites Girgashites Hivites Arkites Sinites Arvadites Zemarites Hamathites
•• Later the Canaanite clans scattered and the borders of Canaan reached from Sidon towards Gerar as far as Gaza and then towards Sodom, Gomorrah, Admah and Zeboiim as far as Lasha.			

Imagine

The story of the flood and the enormous boat that Noah built lived on in folklore. It was a memory that gave birth to an idea.

Many years later the descendants of Ham and Japheth, possibly inspired by the story of Noah and the ark, began to build boats themselves.

The descendants of Ham kept alive the older technique of building boats by binding bundles of reed together. They invented oars and sails and ventured gradually further and further down the Tigris and Euphrates, around the coast of the Persian Gulf and into the Red Sea from whence they carried their small boats overland to relaunch them in the Nile and the Mediterranean.

Meanwhile, Japheth's offspring, some of whom had settled along the coast of what we now know as Turkey and Syria, were also venturing into boatbuilding, using timber and daubing it with bitumen as Noah had done with the ark. From settlements along the Mediterranean coast they began to launch, first small fishing boats, and then larger and larger constructions that could carry substantial cargoes along the coast from village to village.

These early sailors hugged the shore, though they knew how to navigate using the stars at night. Some were caught by storms and blown out to sea out of sight of land. Some were drowned. Others found themselves stranded on far-off, deserted coasts, they didn't know where. And still others came ashore on islands like Crete, Cyprus and Rhodes from which they were able to find their way back home.

They established settlements on these islands and along the coasts of the Mediterranean and brought back fruit, olive oil, wine and timbers and spices and metals which they traded with people in other communities, becoming wealthy as a result.

In time, some of the sons of Japheth sailed all the way to the south of Spain, reaching the gateway to the Atlantic Ocean, where one of them established a town and seaport near what we now know as Gibraltar. He named it after himself. Tarsessus, or Tarshish.

It was a daring step to sail out through the straits and into the ocean beyond but eventually someone had the courage to do it and the descendants of Japheth then began to spread northwards along the coasts of Spain and France, into Brittany, along the English Channel into Normandy, across to Cornwall and on to Ireland. Legend has it that, many, many generations later, a descendant of Japheth called Brutus gave his name to the island that the Romans eventually knew as Brutannia (or Britain, as we call it today).

The first drunk

Tarshish became a thriving port, the gateway to a new world. Ships arrived there from Ireland and Cornwall, carrying wool and tin and precious metals. Others arrived from the distant east, carrying spices and silks and cedarwood and precious stones. Still more came up the coast of Africa, laden with coconut, ivory and strange exotic fruits. Cargoes were unloaded, traded, reloaded, transported back to distant countries. Sailors from all over the known world met in Tarshish and talked and exchanged tales of their homelands and speculated as to what dangers, mysteries or adventures might lie beyond the Atlantic horizon that none of them dared to cross.

Information

Ham had four sons, Cush, Mizraim, Put and Canaan. Each gave his name to a nation or race of people descended from him.

The descendants of Cush populated the area sometimes known as Mesopotamia, the huge plain between the rivers Tigris and Euphrates. Some of them travelled by boat round the Persian Gulf and down the coast of Africa, populating the areas we now know as Somalia, Eritrea and Ethiopia.

The descendants of Mizraim also migrated by sea round the Persian Gulf and began to populate the area now covered by Egypt. Mizraim is still the name of Egypt in the Hebrew language.

The descendants of Put also migrated into Egypt but occupied the north of the country around the Nile delta and then spread along the Mediterranean coast of Africa.

The descendants of Canaan, the fourth son, migrated westwards from Mesopotamia, overland, across the Arabian desert to the area now covered by Palestine, Jordan and Israel.

Chapter 11

The first empire

The sons of Ham by their clans and languages in their territories and nations

Scripture (Genesis 10 v 9–12)

Nimrod grew to be a mighty hunter before the Lord. Hence the saying, "Like Nimrod, a mighty hunter before the Lord." The first centres of his kingdom were Babylon, Shinar, Akkad or Calneh in Shinar. From that land he went to Assyria where he built Nineveh, Rehoboth, Ir, Calah and Resen which is between Nineveh and Calah, that is, the great city.

Imagine

The long procession wound its way along the rugged path through the mountains. Soldiers with breastplates and scarlet tunics, mounted on horses, rode in the front and back of the convoy. Between the two troops of cavalry, hundreds of pack animals, mules and camels, plodded along, struggling with their heavy load of supplies. In the centre, mounted on a camel, was a man dressed in fine robes. A leather satchel was slung over his shoulder which he touched, nervously, from time to time.

It was not the first time that the royal emissary of King Nimrod, the Mighty Hunter, had made the long journey from Uruk in the south of Mesopotamia along the course of the great river Euphrates into the Zagros mountains and onward through several more mountain passes to the mountain kingdom of Ararat. Correspondence had been taking place for several years between King Nimrod and the King of Ararat and it was his privilege and burden to be the emissary between them.

The sun was beginning to sink on the horizon and it was essential they made it to the Royal palace before it set. They could do it, if they kept up a good pace. He sent a servant running along to the front of the convoy, urging everyone to move faster.

Information

Archaeologist David Rohl identifies the Biblical King Nimrod as the Sumerian King Enmerkar who ruled from a city called Uruk (the name survives today, now applied to a whole country, Iraq). Uruk was the Sumerian name for this city. In another language of the time, Akkadian, it was also known as Nun Ki. The Akkadian people also used the same name, Nun Ki, for another town, one which the Sumerians called Babilu.

Nimrod, or Enmerkar, to give him his Sumerian name, was the first empire builder on record in human history, conquering other kings and making them and their territories subject to him. Documents survive from a long correspondence which Enmerkar/Nimrod carried on with Ensukushsiranna, the ruler of Aratta. In the letters Nimrod made a series of ever more complex demands with the threat of invasion if these were not carried out. In the end Nimrod did invade and conquered Aratta, making it part of his empire.

The first empire

The Mountain Kingdom of Ararat, founded originally by Noah himself, had become fabulously wealthy. In no other nation on earth were the people so happy and well fed. It was a pleasant and fertile land which could produce almost everything it needed. The prosperity of the kingdom was assured by the gold, silver and copper that was mined in the depths of the mountains.

But the kingdom of Uruk had also grown wealthy and strong. Its situation couldn't be more different from that of Ararat. It was built on the Mesopotamian Plain not too far North of the Persian Gulf. For centuries the two kingdoms had flourished and grown separately, each aware of the other but with little interaction between them. More recently the megalomaniac tendencies of Nimrod had changed the relationship. Nimrod was the son of Cush, the son of Ham. Systematically, he had picked quarrels with the kings of other nations and used them as a pretext to send in his highly trained army to conquer and plunder them and to bring them into submission. Gradually, the whole of the vast plain between the Tigris and the Euphrates had come under his domination. He had also sent settlers into areas of low population in Assyria and established new cities, among them Nineveh, Cala and Resen.

Ararat, with its mountainous position and fabulous riches, was a tougher nut to crack. But Nimrod was eager to add this prize to his collection. He was demanding that the king of Ararat acknowledge allegiance to him and pay a tax to show his loyalty. The Envoy had taken the same message several times. Each time the answer had been "No." Each time Nimrod countered with a list of conditions that got longer and more complex. At least, this time, thanks to the invention of writing, the Envoy wouldn't have to memorise it all. The details were all carefully inscribed in the clay tablet tucked in his satchel. He touched it again, to make sure it was safe. As he did they rounded a curve and he could see the walls of the city ahead of him. What reception would they receive this time?

Chapter 12

The first communication crisis
(The clans of Noah's sons according to their lines of descent)

Scripture (Genesis 11 v 1–8)

Now there was a situation where the whole earth had a common language and spoke the same way.

As people migrated eastward they found a plain in the land of Shinar and settled there. They spoke to one another and said, "Let's make bricks and bake them hard." They used brick instead of stone and bitumen instead of mortar. Then they said, "Let's build for ourselves a city with a tower that has its top in the heavens so that we may make a name for ourselves and not be scattered over the surface of the earth."

Then Jahweh came down to look at the city and the tower that they were busily building. Jahweh said, "If this is what they have begun to do when they are united and speaking one language, nothing they put their minds to will be impossible for them. Come, let's go down and confuse their speech so they will not understand each other's language."

Information

It's easy to read into the Bible things that aren't there. Sometimes it's because our own imagination is filling in the gaps. Sometimes it's because we have seen illustrations or paintings of Bible stories or we've heard preachers describe what's in the Bible narrative.

The story of the tower of Babel is a good case in point. Did you imagine that the completed tower came tumbling down as God sent a thunderbolt from heaven? It doesn't say that in the Bible. Genesis says God scattered the people and they stopped building. Did you imagine that the builders all suddenly started speaking different languages and couldn't understand one another? You can interpret the Bible that way. But it could just as well have been that, from that point on, separate languages began to develop.

In my reconstruction, I've followed the theory that Nimrod was the same person as the Sumerian ruler Enmerkar and that his capital city was the same as the place called Babel in the Bible.

Often, with political events recorded in the Bible, there are two levels of causation, a cause that happens on a natural level (for example the defeat of a king in battle caused by the brilliant strategy of his opponent) and another cause that is on a supernatural level (the defeated king is under God's judgement because of his sin). The Bible and Sumerian literature agree that the work on the tower stopped because Nimrod, or Enmerkar, had brought divine displeasure on himself. The archaeological evidence confirms that work on a huge tower in Enmerkar's capital came to a halt. We don't know whether it was the death of Nimrod, a lack of funds or a disaster of some kind that stopped the work.

The first communication crisis

So Yahweh scattered them from there over all the surface of the Earth and they stopped building the city. That's why it was given the name of Babel, because from there God mixed up their speech and they began to babble in different languages as Jahweh scattered them all over the Earth's surface.

Imagine

The King of Aratta once more refused Nimrod's long list of "peace" conditions. The Envoy travelled back, fearfully, to report this stubbornness to his master. Nimrod mobilised his armies and, helped by his son, Lugumbanda, mounted a campaign to conquer the territories beyond the northern mountains. The campaign was successful and they eventually returned, bringing back a huge hoard of gems and precious metals and a statue of the goddess Inana.

With Aratta subdued, Nimrod needed new ways to express his megalomaniac tendencies. He was now the ruler of a vast empire. He needed a capital city and a home that adequately expressed his importance. He became obsessed with the fact that Aratta, although defeated, was a mountain kingdom and was thence higher then his home city of Uruk. He was nervous, also, that the mountain goddess Inana would not feel at home in the flat plains of his kingdom and, being unhappy, would turn against him.

His solution was to build a little mountain within his capital city. It would stretch up into the sky and be topped by a huge temple to Inana. They didn't have rock to build with but the Sumerians had become skilled in making and using bricks. He began to build a huge, brick platform.

When the platform was eventually complete, Nimrod arranged for a temple to be built on the front of the platform to their own local god, Enki. But, behind Enki's temple a further platform reached up to an even higher level. The plan was to put a temple to Inana at its summit.

But the temple to Inana was never built. For some reasonm, the worked stopped.

About the same time, people began to notice that, as they spread out over the earth, people's speech patterns began to grow apart. When the people of one area travelled to visit people in another area, they found they could no longer understand what foreigners were saying, nor make themselves understood.

It became a talking point, a bit like global warming today. One husband and wife were so concerned about it that they called their son "Peleg" meaning "division" because, as they saw it, the human race was splitting apart.

The Bible and the Sumerian literature agree that it was divine judgement for Nimrod's exaggerated pride that caused the multiplication of languages.

Languages

Languages are shaped by two opposing pressures, the need to communicate, which makes people speak in the same way, and on the other hand the laziness (or creativity) that makes individuals say things differently. When a language community is split by politics, geography or migration, the same language will gradually change in the two groups, accents and dialects developing that eventually devolve into completely separate languages. Differences between American, Australian and British English illustrate this perfectly. The writer of the account of the Tower of Babel regards this tendency for languages to split as a protective obstacle that God introduced to avoid human cleverness getting out of hand.

The official, establishment, scientific view is that language evolved gradually as the human race developed from ape-like ancestors. But that raises some questions. If language, and hence the human race, developed so slowly over millions of years, how come the world didn't become overpopulated long ago? And if language developed gradually, you might expect older languages to be simple, primitive and irregular and more recent ones to be complex, and structured and more regular. In fact, the trend is the other way. Ancient, classical languages are regular and highly structured. Modern languages are simpler and less tidy, with more irregular forms.

Chapter 13

Life flows on
(The record of Shem combined with
The sons of Shem by their clans and languages in
their territories and nations)

Scripture

You'll find the scripture passages laid out in the form of a table on the next two pages.

Information

As the oldest son, Shem inherited the kingdom of his father, Noah. This may be why all the other sons moved outwards to start settlements elsewhere. The territory populated by Shem's offspring included the area in the Zagros mountains where the ark had come to rest and the territories closest to it, including most of the territories in the middle east, modern day Persia, Iraq, Turkey and Syria, along with Palestine, Jordan and Israel.

The sons of Shem in their territories and nations
(Genesis 10 v 21–31)

Elam	Asshur	Arphaxad		Lud	Aram
		Shelah			Uz Hul Gether Meshech
		Eber			
		Peleg ("division") - so named because in his time the earth was divided.	Joktan		
			Almodad Sheleph Hazarmaveth Jerah Hadoram Uzai Diktah Obal Abimael Sheba Ophir Havilah Jobab (The region where they lived stretched from Mesha towards Sephar in the eastern hill country).		

Life flows on

The Record of Shem
(Genesis 11 v 10–26)

Two years after the flood, when Shem was 100 years old, he became the father of Arphaxad.

Name of descendant	Age at birth of first son	Name of first son	Other children	Further years to death	Age at death
Shem	100	Arphaxad	Other sons and daughters	500	600
Arphaxad	35	Shelah	Other sons and daughters	403	438
Shelah	30	Eber	Other sons and daughters	403	433
Eber	34	Peleg	Other sons and daughters	430	464
Peleg	30	Reu	Other sons and daughters	209	239
Reu	32	Serug	Other sons and daughters	206	238
Serug	30	Nahor	Other sons and daughters	200	230
Nahor	29	Terah	Other sons and daughters	119	148
Terah	70	Abram	Nahor and Haran	205	275

Information

Pot-holing is not my idea of fun. But once the pot-holers have done their exploring and someone has cut passages high enough to walk through without banging your head, and laid decent footpaths and installed electric light, I find it an interesting experience to admire the amazing underground world that the pot-holers have discovered. It fascinates me to see how how small rivers can dive underground and carve their way through tunnels and caves, to rush out into the sunlight again miles downstream.

Sometimes the Holy Spirit acts like an underground river. For years, there's little of God's work to see. And then it's as if God bursts out into the sunlight again.

Two of the clay documents that were merged into Genesis are a bit like that. One short one has a long title, "These are the sons of Shem by their clans and languages in their territories and nations". The other is simply entitled "This is the account of Shem". Both are just a list of names. They tell us that, two years after the flood, Shem had a son called Arphaxad. Then they just list the family line down to a man called Terah. Apart from a brief note to explain why Peleg got his name, they tell us nothing about the people named, who they were, where they lived or what they did.

We do know that, when Shem's wife gave birth to Arphaxad, they would have still been living in the Zagros mountains, in modern day Turkey, near to where the ark had come to rest. It's with Terah, at the end of the list, that the underground stream bubbles up into the light of day. Terah has a separate document all to

Life flows on

himself. When we first meet him, he is living in a city called Ur, 1,000 miles away on the Euphrates delta in an area that now lies within Iraq. In the intervening generations, the family have spread out, multiplied, drifted downstream from the mountains to the Persian Gulf and covered the land with cities. The account of Shem lists ordinary people who went about their ordinary lives, passing on the stories of the flood and the people who lived before it and passing on their faith in the God who specially created Adam and used to talk to him in the cool of the evening.

Did God try to speak to any of them? Did they try to speak to God, or listen out for his voice? We don't know.

How close does God feel to you? If he seems far away, is it because you haven't tried to make contact with him? Are you carrying on your daily routine, leaving God out of it? Is God waiting for someone to come along who will turn their attention towards him? Could that be you?

Of course, it may be that you're living in one of God's underground periods. Could you be a vital link in a chain, passing on the treasures of the faith to your children and preparing the way for someone in the future who will grasp the heritage you've passed on and become someone significant in God's sight?

Chapter 14

The first step on the road to the promised land
(The record of Terah)

Scripture (Genesis 11 v 27–32)

Terah became the father of Abram, Nahor and Haran.

Haran had a son called Lot. Haran died in his father's presence in the land where he was born, in Ur of the Chaldaeans.

Haran's brothers, Abram and Nahor, both took wives. The name of Abram's wife was Sarai. Sarai was Abram's half sister, the daughter of Terah by a previous marriage. Nahor married Milcah, who was the daughter of Haran and hence Nahor's neice. Haran also had another daughter, Iscah. Sarai was barren, she had no children.

Terah took Abram, his son, Lot, his grandson, and Sarai, Abram's bride and wife, and they all set out from Ur of the Chaldaeans to go to Canaan. But when they came to Haran, they settled there.

Terah lived 205 years and he died in Haran.

Imagine

"What's the matter, my dear, have I done something to upset you?"

Terah's wife had been giving off negative signals all day. Terah was beginning to realise that something was wrong.

"There's so much to do!" she exclaimed, "I've got to collect the washing from the laundry, I've got to take your clay tablets back to the library; I want to go and say goodbye to the neighbours and I'll need to go to the market, and the butchers – there are so many things we need for the journey."

"We'll pass by market places on the way. We only need food for one or two days," Terah replied.

"But I still need to clean the house, I want to leave it in perfect condition for Nahor and Milcah."

"Just tell me what to do, and I'll speak to Nahor and Abram and ask them to speak to Lot and Sarai and get them to help you. Young Ischa can lend a hand as well."

She burst into tears. Terah stepped over to comfort her. She buried her head in his shoulder but then thumped his chest with her fists.

"Why do we have to go? We've been so happy here in Ur. We've got everything we need here."

"I've told you, my darling. God has spoken to us. You agreed when I first told you. It's not as if I've forced it on you. God's going to lead us to a new land where we can make a new start. We're going to go somewhere where the grass is green and there are hundreds of trees laden with fruit, a place where we can raise livestock and have fresh food; somewhere where we can live in freedom the way Jahweh wants us to, without the pressure to worship the moon goddess like everyone else."

She dried her eyes.

"I know," she said. "I'll be alright, once we're on our way. But I'm going to miss all the friends we've made here."

Information

The relationships in Terah's family were complex. Terah had been married once before and was now married a second time. With his second wife he had a daughter, Sarai. Terah also had had three sons by his first marriage, Abram, Nahor and Haran. Abram married his half sister, Sarai. Haran married and had a son, Lot, and two daughters, Milcah and Ischa. Later, he died. Milcah married her uncle, Nahor.

Abram and Sarai travelled with Terah and his wife when they left Ur. So did Haran's son Lot, his wife and his daughter, Ischa. But Nahor and Milchah stayed in Ur.

With over 64,000 inhabitants, Ur was in those days the largest city on earth. At the time, it was on the shore of the Persian Gulf, near the mouth of the great River Euphrates (the site now lies several miles inland). It was a rich and prosperous port, a comfortable place to live in many ways but it also suffered from all the problems of city life, including crime and disease. For Terah and his family who worshipped Jahweh, the creator God, life there was also difficult because every aspect of life in Ur was involved with the worship of the moon goddess whose huge temple dominated the city.

Terah and his wife were about to leave Ur and migrate north. He wanted to visit the area where his ancestors had once lived. From there, they would seek Jahweh's guidance and, hopefully, find somewhere to settle permanently. They planned possibly to move on into Canaan, following the line of the fertile crescent in search of a good place to set up home. It involved a huge change of lifestyle for them. For all their lives they had lived in brick built houses. Now they were going to sleep in tents. Their preparations for the journey had been very thorough. They had all they could possibly need and the pack animals to carry it. But it was still an enormous adventure and, now that the time to leave was approaching, Terah's wife was finding it hard to cope with the grief and fear which kept overwhelming her.

The day came. They said their goodbyes and set out. They travelled northwards along the river Euphrates and eventually found a place to settle.

In time they established a village which later grew to a town. By then Terah and his wife had had enough of travel. They settled down in Haran, and put down roots. Terah died there.

Information

In most English translations it looks as if Terah's son Haran has the same name as the town where Terah died but in Hebrew the names are different. The place is pronounced with a fricative sound like the ch in a Scottish loch – "Charan." It means either "glowing" or "scorched". The name of Terah's son has a normal, softer "h". His name is intriguing, though. In Ur of the Chaldees, surrounded by the flat plains of the Euphrates delta, Terah gave his son a name which means "mountaineer".

The first step on the road to the promised land

Information

That's where the clay tablets come to an end but someone else took up the story and you can continue reading it in the Bible from Genesis 12 onwards. Abram became the father of both the Jewish and Arab races. He is honoured by both Jews and Muslims. Christians, too, regard him as their forefather because of the verse in Paul's letter to the Romans where he says that Abram is "the father of all who believe but have not been circumcised, in order that righteousness might be credited to them."

Imagine

"It's quite a collection, isn't it?" says the scribe.

"It certainly is," we agree. "Are these all the clay tablets you have? Are there any more?"

"I'm afraid these are all I have," he says. "I got them from Nahor. I'm glad his father made it to Haran. I wonder what's happened to Abram and Lot?"

"Shall I tell him?" I think, and look to you for guidance. We make eye contact, both give a surreptitious shake of our heads to signal that we have agreed to keep quiet. Talking of the future to people in the past could lead to all kinds of problems.

"They'll be fine, as long as they are faithful to Jahweh." I say. "Thank you for showing us your clay tablets. Writing is a fantastic invention."

And we walk back to our time machine.

Notes for group discussion

You might like to use *First Things First* in the context of a small group study, a Lent course or a reading circle. These notes are designed to help group leaders in these contexts. Get group members to read the appropriate chapter during the preceding week and then use the ideas in these notes to stimulate discussion, prayer and action. If you use every chapter, the notes will give you a 12 week study. For those who need a shorter course, for example for Lent, the notes divide the book into two sections. You can use either of these sections to form a shorter, 6 week Lent course.

Section 1

Stories from the dawn of time

Week 1

Chapter 1 – In the first place (Genesis 1 v 1–2 v 3)

What does Genesis 1 tell you about God's relationship with the universe?

What does it tell you about your own relationship with the natural world?

What do you think about the suggestion that creation is still going on and that we are currently in day 6 with a future Sabbath yet to come?

Whether you see the Sabbath day as commemorating the completion of creation or looking forward to it, the author of Genesis 1 obviously views the Sabbath day as important and holy. "Remember the Sabbath day to keep it holy" is one of the ten commandments. How important should the Sabbath be to us? Does the Christian Sunday equate to the Jewish Sabbath?

What should keeping the Sabbath holy mean for us today?

Under what circumstances would it be right or wrong for a Christian to work on a Sunday?

Action
What action can your group take to express respect for creation and for the Sabbath?

Prayer suggestion
Give thanks for the natural world and pray for those seeking to establish a sustainable future (from politicians through campaigners to charities working to preserve endangered species).

Week 2

Chapter 2 – The first man (Genesis 2 v 4–17)

What was special about the garden?

What was special about the man?

What does the passage tell us about our relationship with the animal world?

How should we view animals? As pets, endangered species, or food?

Action
How can your group express a Christian concern for the animal world? Why not get information and do something in support of an animal charity such as World Wildlife Fund (WWF), Royal Society for the Protection of Birds (RSPB) or the Royal Society for the Protection of Animals (RSPCA?

Prayer suggestion
Give thanks for the animals that members of the group are responsible for (pets, livestock, birds that visit your garden, etc).

Pray for people who make a living through animal husbandry and for organisations that promote animal welfare.

Week 3

Chapter 3 – The first woman (Genesis 2 v 21–3 v 24)

Whenever Jesus or Paul talked about marriage they referred back to this passage. What does this passage teach us about marriage? Read the following passages that refer back to this passage in Genesis:

Malachi 2 v 13–16
Matthew 19 v 6
Mark 10 v 2–9
1 Corinthians 6 v 16
Ephesians 5 v 28–32

How do they add to our understanding of marriage?

In Malachi v 2 v 16 God says "I hate divorce." That doesn't mean that God hates the people who divorce their partners or who are divorced. It is the act of divorce that he hates because he knows what it does to the people involved. However, it does mean that divorce is something to consider only as a last resort.

How can we make sure that Christian marriages remain strong?

How can we help those who are facing the break up of their marriage?

The issues between Adam and Eve are about intimacy and cunning (intimacy in the sense of open sharing of innermost thoughts and emotions). How easy do you find it to maintain intimacy in relationships with friends or members of your family? What makes us reluctant to be intimate?

Are there circumstances in which too much intimacy between two people might be dangerous?

What problems are likely to occur where cunning is a major aspect of our relationship with someone?

Action:
Make a donation or organise a fund raising activity to support a charity or counselling service that works to strengthen marriages or family life.

Prayer suggestion
Pray for the marriages represented in your group and for people who are working to strengthen marriages.

Pray for any you know who are going through marriage break up or rebuilding their lives afterwards.

Week 4

**Chapter 4 – The first murder (Genesis 4 v 1–17)
and Chapter 5 – The first city (Genesis 4 v 17–26)**

Chapter 4 – The first murder (Genesis 4 v 1–17)

What was wrong with Cain's offering? Why was Abel's better?

Can you think of situations in your life where your emotional reactions have been similar to those of Cain (envy, anger, feeling rejected). What does the story of Cain and Abel have to say to help those who have these reactions?

God doesn't give up on Cain. He continues to care for him, even when he is facing the unpleasant consequences of his sin. How does God show his continuing care for Cain?

Chapter 5 – The first city (Genesis 4 v 17–26)
How do Cain's attitudes, and his sinful behaviour, reappear later in his family line in the stories of Lamech, Adah and Zillah?

Prayer suggestion
In a silent prayer time, search your hearts and ask God's forgiveness for times when you have given in to resentful, envious or bitter reactions.

Pray for those who are working for peace in parts of the world where there is tension and conflict.

Action
Are there people you need to be reconciled with? Make a step towards reconciliation – a letter perhaps, a phone call, or simply praying for God to give an opportunity for the breach to be repaired.

Week 5

Chapter 6 – The first man dies (Genesis 5 v 1–32)
(Take these two chapters together as one study)

The "imagine" section makes two big assumptions which might not be true:
1. That Adam died before Eve.
2. That the similar names in the two genealogies reflect a reconciliation between Cain's and Seth's family lines as a result of which Seth's descendants name their children after some of the people in Cain's line.

How would Adam have felt if Eve had died first?

What was special about Enoch? How is he an example for us to follow? What do you think it means to "walk with God."

What experiences of grief have people in your group had? How have they coped with grief?

Talk about your heritage. Do people in the group have an inspiring heritage? How do your ancestors affect your self image?

Action/Prayer suggestions
Give thanks for your parents, grandparents and ancestors and for any positive, godly influences they have had on you. Ask God to forgive them for any sins they committed and to release you from any negative effects that their behaviour has had on your family line.

Pray for your descendants and ask God to help you to pass on a beneficial heritage to them.

Week 6

Chapter 7 – The first superheroes (Genesis 6 v 1-8)
Chapter 8 – The first ocean voyage (Genesis 6 v 9–7 v 24)
(Take these two chapters together as one study)

What do you think about the four theories about Genesis 6 v 1 – 8?

"But God saw that the wickedness of mankind was great in the earth and his thoughts were inclined to evil all day long. He regretted that he had made man in the earth and his heart was filled with pain." What do you think God might think of the human race today? Is there anything that has happened in the meantime that might have changed God's attitude?

What was special about Noah? How did God respond to it? What can we learn from Noah's example?

Universal flood or a localised one – what do you think?

Action
Read the New Testament references to the flood together and discuss what you can learn from them.

Matthew 24 v 37, 38
Luke 17 v 26, 27
Hebrews 11 v 7
1 Peter 3 v 20
2 Peter 2 v 5

If you have chosen to do a six week course using section 1, this is where the course ends.

Section 2
Noah and now

You can start here if you want to do a short course based on Genesis 8 -11

Week 7 (Week 1)

Chapter 9 – The first covenant (Genesis 8 v 20– 9 v 17)

What is the significance of the rainbow, in Biblical terms?

Read and discuss the passages that refer to the covenants God makes.

What difference does it make to know that God makes covenants and keeps them?

As believers, how can we show others that we are children of a covenant- keeping God?

Prayer suggestion
Give thanks for God's faithfulness.

Week 8 (Week 2)

Chapter 10 – The first drunk (Genesis 9 v 18–10 v 7)

The scripture passages for this study raise issues that challenge things we take for granted in our culture - attitudes to nakedness and attitudes to alcohol and other mind or mood altering substances. There is an interesting contrast between Adam and Eve who were "naked and unashamed" and Noah, whose nakedness brings shame on him and on his sons. What has happened to bring about the change in attitudes to nakedness? Do you think there is more at stake here than just the absence of clothes?

How does our society's attitude to nakedness differ (if at all) from that of Noah and his sons? Different cultures even today have different rules (contrast the middle eastern burkah and topless bathing at Mediterranean resorts). What are the issues at stake and do you think the culture you are part of has it right or wrong?

Does our society have a healthy attitude to alcohol?

How as Christians should we respond to the misuse of drugs?

"None of the heroes of faith was perfect." What encouragement can we gain from this fact?

Action
Find out what organisations are working to help with drug and alcohol abuse in your community and whether they need any financial or practical help.

Prayer
Pray for the people involved on both sides of these organisations (helping and being helped).

Week 9 (Week 3)

Chapter 11 – The first empire (Genesis 10 v 8–12)

Nimrod, "a mighty hunter before the Lord" – Nimrod was possibly the world's first aggressive, autocratic, empire building dictator. He was the father of people like Nebuchadnezzar, Alexander, the Roman Caesars, Genghis Khan, Napoleon Bonaparte and Adolf Hitler.

What makes someone become a despotic empire-builder?

How do we feel about Britain's imperial past?

The same spirit that drove the great despotic rulers of history may also motivate lesser people who want to throw their weight around in a work, church or neighbourhood context. How can we recognise when that spirit is at work and how should we respond?

What can we do to prevent new Nimrods from gaining power and influence?

Action
Find out about people who are living under despotic regimes to day. Take any political action you may feel appropriate, for example:

- praying for them
- making a donation or holding a fund raising event for Amnesty International or a Christian organisation working in the same field
* lobbying to bring their case to the attention of governments that might be able to change their situation.

Week 10 (Week 4)

Chapter 12 – The first communications crisis (Genesis 11 v 1–8)

The people who built the tower of Babel planned to build a tower whose top was in the skies. What do you think this story has to say to a generation who have visited the moon and sent probes to the outer reaches of the solar system?

Which was God judging, the technological achievement of the citizens of Babel or the motivation of their hearts?

Bible Study

Follow the theme of language through the Bible, looking at the following passages. Note down any thoughts that occur to you and any interesting connections you make.

Bible passages on the theme of language
John 1 v 1–5
Genesis 11 v 1–9
Isaiah 28 v 11
John 19 v 19–20
Acts 2 v 1–12
1 Corinthians 12 v 14–25
Revelation 5 v 9
Revelation 7 v 9

Action/ Prayer suggestion
Pray for people involved in scientific and technological research. Some research can throw up difficult ethical issues. Pray for scientists, theologians and ethicists as they tackle these issues.

Week 11 (Week 5)

Chapter 13 – Life flows on (Genesis 10 v 21–11 v 26

Life isn't always exciting and eventful. Ordinary people get on with their ordinary lives for year after year, century after century.

How do ordinary days affect our faith and our relationship with God?

If ordinary days have a negative impact on our faith, what can we do to keep our faith strong when nothing much is happening?

Action

Get each person in your group to share what an ordinary day is like for them and use this as a basis for praying for each other.

Week 13 (Week 6)

Chapter 14 – First steps on the road to the promised land (Genesis 11 v 27–32)

We live in a mobile society where many people live a semi-nomadic life, moving from place to place or commuting large distances to find work. Immigration and emigration are also part of this picture. The story of Terah and his family shows that the mobile society is nothing new. Their experience of uprooting themselves to find a new home is one many today can identify with.

What is the experience of your group? Are you all typical of this trend or not?

What are the pros and cons of a mobile society?

What are the implications for the church of witnessing in a mobile society? How does a constantly changing congregation affect a local church's witness, growth and fellowship and how can local congregations adapt?

Can you think of some good reasons for moving to a new home and maybe some that might be not so good?

Action
Think of ways that you as a group or a church can make newcomers to your local community feel welcome. Make some plans and carry them out.

Sources

The following books have contributed in different ways to shape my understanding of Genesis 1–11.

Genesis, An Introduction and Commentary by Derek Kidner, Tyndale Press.
Genesis in Space and Time by Francis A Schaeffer published by Hodder.
Nelson's Illustrated Bible Dictionary, published by Thomas Nelson.
The Lost Testament by David Rohl, published by Century, Random House UK Ltd.
Word Biblical Commentary, Genesis 1–15 by Gordon Wenham, published by Word inc.